National
Theatre
Wales

Joseph K and the Cost of Living

by/gan Emily White

T0333382

Joseph K and the Cost of Living was produced by National Theatre Wales and first performed at Swansea Grand Theatre in March 2023 as part of three-part production called *The Cost of Living*.

Cynhyrchwyd *Joseph K and the Cost of Living* gan National Theatre Wales a'i berfformio am y tro cyntaf yn Theatr y Grand Abertawe yn mis Mawrth 2023 fel rhan o gynhyrchiad tair rhan o'r enw *The Cost of Living*.

Joseph K and the Cost of Living
by/gan Emily White

Cast

Joni Ayton-Kent	K2, Colleague 1, Busker, Student, Voice, Banker, Tenant, Protestor
Sara Beer	Ms Grubach, Banker, Fruit Seller, Magistrate, Water Seller, Block, Voice, Tenant, Protestor
Rahim El Habachi	Elsa, Preacher 1, Whipper, Giuseppe, Cleaner, Man, Voice, Banker, Tenant, Protestor
Lucy Ellinson	K3, Titorelli, Guard 1, Petitioner 1, Tenant 2, Sex Worker, Karla, Banker, Tenant, Woman, Protestor
Gruffudd Glyn	Joseph K1, Leni, Banker, Tenant, Protestor
Ioan Hefin	Guard 2, Bank Manager, Preacher 2, Police, Huld, Chaplain, Voice, Banker, Tenant, Protestor
Anthony Matsena	Investigator, Colleague 1, Tenant 3, Volunteer, Clerk, Andrew Tate, Glitterman, Homeless Dancer, Voice, Banker, Tenant, Police, Protestor
Kel Matsena	K4, Tenant 1, Colleague 2, Petitioner 2, Homeless Dancer, Man, Voice, Banker, Tenant, Protestor

Creative Team

Lorne Campbell	Director / Cyfarwyddwr
Kel Matsena	Co-director / Cyd-gyfarwyddwr
Anthony Matsena	Co-director / Cyd-gyfarwyddwr
Kaite O'Reilly	Dramaturg / Dramatwrg
Hannah Marie Williams	Casting Director / Cyfarwyddwr Castio
Bianca Ali	Assistant Director / Cyfarwyddwr Cynorthwyol
Cai Dyfan	Set and Costume Design / Cynllunydd Set a Gwisgoedd
Jane Lalljee	Lighting Designer / Cynllunydd Goleuo
Alex Comana	Sound Designer / Cynllunydd Sain

Production Team

Nia Thomson	Production Manager / Rheolwr Cynhyrchu
Weronika Szumelda	Assistant Production Manager / Rheolwr Cynhyrchu Cynorthwyol
Linda Fitzpatrick	Company Stage Manager / Rheolwr Llwyfan y Cwmni
Theo Hung	Deputy Stage Manager / Dirprwy Reolwr Llwyfan
Devon James-Bowen	Assistant Stage Manager / Rheolwr Llwyfan Cynorthwyol
Jon Cox	Sound System Designer / Cynllunydd System Sain
Josh Bowles	Sound Technician and Operator / Technegydd a Gweithredwr Sain
Cara Hood	Lighting Technician and Operator / Technegydd a Gweithredwr Goleuo
Amy Barratt	Costume Supervisor / Goruchwyliwr Gwisgoedd
Luned Evans	Design Assistant / Cynorthwyydd Dylunio
Bridget Morris	Casting Director Assistant / Cyfarwyddwr Castio Cynorthwyol
Cathy Piquemal	Access Coordinator / Cydlynydd Mynediad
Bronwen Wilson	Wellbeing Coordinator / Cydlynydd Llesiant

Biographies / Bywgraffiadau

Joni Ayton-Kent | Cast

Most notable theatre credits include: *The Prince* (Southwark Playhouse), *Revolt. She Said. Revolt Again* (The Other Room, Cardiff), *A Christmas Carol* (Nottingham Playhouse and Alexandra Palace), *Carousel* (Regents Park Open Air Theatre), *Sweet Charity* (Donmar Warehouse) and *Mermaids* (King's Head Theatre).

Screen work includes: series regular role of Corporal Cheery in *The Watch* (BBC America), series regular Bradley in *Don't Forget the Driver* (BBC), *Lessons* (short film written, directed and produced by Joni), *The Romanoffs* (Amazon), *Misnomer* (short film), and live-action video game *The Isle Tide Hotel* (Wales Interactive) due for release this year.

Sara Beer | Cast

Sara began her acting career with Graeae Theatre Company in London over 30 years ago. Sara worked for Disability Arts Cymru for 15 years, supporting disabled artists across Wales, running projects and creating showcasing opportunities.

Sara has collaborated with Kaite O'Reilly since 2008 on a variety of projects, including the original UK *'d' Monologues*, produced by National Theatre Wales in 2012 where Sara was the emerging director for *In Water I'm Weightless*; performing in *Cosy* at the Wales Millennium Centre and for Gaitkrash Theatre Company in Cork, Ireland and in O'Reilly's Unlimited International Commission, *And Suddenly I Disappear, the Singapore 'd' monologues*, both directed by Phillip Zarrilli.

In 2018, Sara collaborated again with O'Reilly and Zarrilli on *Richard III redux*, creating a one-woman show that provided an opportunity to explore topics close to Sara's heart which initially toured Wales and has since been performed in Germany, Barcelona and in 2022 at the Teatro de la Comedia in Madrid.

Rahim El Habachi | Cast

Rahim is a playwright, actor, belly dancer and activist: in short: Artivist. Originally from Morocco he merges his Moroccan culture with a western flare to create his work. He is a strong advocate for creating spaces and opportunities for creatives from a wide range of backgrounds.

Rahim is currently the Creative Associate with National Theatre Wales. In this role, he has recently co-developed work with Fuel Theatre entitled *Fly the Flag*; exploring the meaning of protest with young people from underrepresented communities in Pembrokeshire. He is also the co-creator of the LGBTQAI+ platform for new writing *Out-Rage-Us*, bringing together NTW, Sherman Theatre, Glitter Cymru and Pride Cymru to place particular focus on those voices which are seen less frequently on our stage, such as those from the global majority and the trans communities.

His previous theatre work includes; *The Love Thief* (writer and performer) for Sherman Theatre, *Beyond The Rainbow* (writer and performer) for Welsh National Opera, and last year's *XXXMAS CAROL* (Big Loop / WMC). He currently has two scripts in development.

Lucy Ellinson | Cast

Lucy is an actor and theatre-maker from Wrecsam. She also teaches, mentors and develops performance, community projects and campaigns.

Current work: International digital collaborations with suite42 (Berlin) *The Sun Sets Eight Times A Day* and *New Digital Gardeners* in partnership with PNT/El Hakawati (Palestine) and Zoukak Theatre (Beirut).

Performer credits include: *Dictating to the Estate* by Nathaniel McBride (Maxilla Social Club, Grenfell, London), *The Thatcher Effect: Beyond Locality* (with Abdalla Daif, DCAF / Cairo), Morgan Lloyd Malcolm's *Typical Girls* (Sheffield Theatres / Clean Break), *Run Sister Run* by Chloë Moss (Sheffield Theatres / Paines Plough), *About Francois* (El Hakawati / suite42), *Macbeth* (Manchester Royal Exchange), Caryl Churchill's *Top Girls*, directed by Lyndsey Turner (National Theatre), Gemma Brockiss and Wendy Hubbard's *Kingdom Come* (RSC, The Other Place), *The Resistible Rise of Arturo Ui* (Donmar) Clare Duffy's *Money: The Game Show* (Bush Theatre), *A Midsummer Night's Dream*, directed by Erica Whyman (RSC National Tour), *Grounded, Trojan Women, Tenet* (Gate Theatre).

Gruffudd Glyn | Cast

Gruffudd trained at the Royal Academy of Dramatic Arts.

Theatre credits include; *Hail Cremation* (National Theatre Wales); *Fantastic Mr Fox* (Lyric Hammersmith/Nuffield), *Brave New World* (Royal & Derngate), *Three Sisters* (Young Vic), *After The End* (Dirty Protest/Sherman Theatre), *American Trade, Hamlet, Romeo and Juliet, Morte D'arthur, The Grainstore, Julius Caesar and The Winter's Tale* (Royal Shakespeare Company) and *Romeo and Juliet* (Theatre of Memory/Middle Temple Hall).

Ioan Hefin | Cast

Theatre credits include: *Tide Whisperer, As Long As The Heart Beats and We're Still Here* (National Theatre Wales), *You Should Ask Wallace, Einstein's Dream* and *The Butterfly Hunter* (Theatr Na n'Og), *The Woman In Black* (Torch Theatre), *Matthew's Passion* (Sherman Cymru), *Aladdin* (RCT), *Y Storm* (Theatr Genedlaethol Cymru), *The Boy Who Went Fishing For Compliments* (Royal Welsh College of Music and Drama) and *Brassed Off* (Clwyd Theatr Cymru).

Anthony Matsena | Co-director / Cyd-gyfarwyddwr and / a cast

Anthony is a Zimbabwean-born and Welsh-raised choreographer, performer and director working between the mediums of dance, theatre, music and poetry. His work often is politically charged, hoping to make sense of his experience of being brought up in an Afrocentric house and having Eurocentric schooling. He has built a love and curiosity for telling stories that express themes of culture, race, change and belonging.

Anthony co-founded Matsena Productions with his brother Kel in 2017 as a reaction to the lack of representation they were seeing in schools, on stage and on screen. They both felt there were very few companies that made work around black stories while using their different skills in African dance, hip-hop, contemporary, rap, theatre and poetry.

Anthony's break-out moment came as a Sadler's Wells Young Associate in 2018, creating works for Lilian Baylis Studio Theatre and the main stage. Recent commissions include Sky Arts, Sadler's Wells, BBC, National Dance Company Wales, Jasmin Vardimon 2, Messums Wiltshire, Royal Welsh College of Music and Drama and CAPA College. He is also an associate artist with National Dance Company Wales and Messums Wiltshire. Anthony sits on the board of National Youth Arts Wales, also chairing the Diversity and Inclusion board for National Youth Dance Wales. Anthony recently became a fellow at Royal Welsh College of Music and Drama.

More recently, he has directed and choreographed *Shades of Blue* which visited Sadler's Wells, DanceEast and RWCMD in Spring 2022 as well as premiering Matsena Productions first feature-length film *Error Code 8:46* in Swansea at Taliesin Arts Centre. Alongside this, his work for National Dance Company of Wales, Codi, toured extensively throughout the UK recently.

Kel Matsena | Co-director / Cyd-gyfarwyddwr and / a cast

Kel is a Zimbabwean-born and Welsh-raised actor, writer and director. Kel began dancing in a street dance trio with his brothers Anthony and Arnold, performing at festivals, charity events and appearing on television. He then began ballet and contemporary dance with Turning Pointe Dance Academy and County Youth Dance Company, later discovering his love for acting at Gower College Swansea.

He graduated from Bristol Old Vic Theatre School and has appeared on television series' for BBC & Channel 4 and feature film *Mad Heidi* as well as *BOING* at Bristol Old Vic and the UK/US Tour of Oliver Award-Winning A Monster Calls. He's worked with Supermassive Games as an actor and mocap performer for multiple games experienced through VR/AR as well as more traditional forms of gaming like Console and PC.

He co-founded Matsena Productions in 2017 with Anthony Matsena and since then they have used the company to create a platform for bolder and more diverse storytelling. He co-wrote *Are You Numb Yet* which won the "International Infallible Award" for "Best Show" at 2020's Digital ED Fringe Festival. This was followed by his co-direction on *Error Code 8:46*, the company's first feature-length film which premiered in Swansea in Spring 2022.

He also appeared in an original BBC documentary, *Brothers in Dance: Anthony and Kel Matsena*, which followed the lives and creative process of Kel and his brother Anthony.

This year he co-directed *DREAM* for Royal Welsh College of Music and Drama and also assisted on the creation of Codi, a new work for National Dance Company Wales which toured the UK extensively. More recently, Kel co-directed and co-choreographed *Shades of Blue* which visited DanceEast, RWCMD and Sadler's Wells, receiving critical acclaim.

Emily White | Writer / Awdur

Emily is an emerging screenwriter and playwright. Her acclaimed play, *Pavilion*, premiered at Theatr Clwyd in 2019, directed by Tamara Harvey and was published by Faber & Faber.

In 2020 she was nominated as Theatr Clwyd's writer for the English Touring Theatre program, *Nationwide Voices* and was also commissioned by Theatr Clwyd to write her play *Atlantis*, which went on to win the George Devine Award for most promising playwright.

She also has television and film projects in development with the BBC and Riot Time Pictures.

Lorne Campbell | Director / Cyfarwyddwr

Lorne is Artistic Director of National Theatre Wales. Lorne began his career at the Traverse Theatre in Edinburgh Prior to joining NTW he was Artistic Director of Northern Stage. Highlights of his time at Northern Stage include *The Bloody Great Border Ballad* (2015) *Get Carter* (2016) and *The Last Ship* (2018), and Northern Stage's multi-award winning showcasing work at the Edinburgh Fringe.

Prior to Northern Stage, Campbell worked as a freelance theatre director creating productions for Liverpool Everyman and Playhouse Theatres, Birmingham Rep, Theatre Royal Bath, Traverse Theatre, The Almeida and Hull Truck. He was Associate Director at the Traverse Theatre between 2004 and 2008. He worked as a Course Director at Drama Centre and as a Creative Fellow of the RSC between 2011 and 2013 and as founding co-Artistic Director of Greyscale between 2009 and 2013.

Kaite O'Reilly | Dramaturg / Dramatwrg

Kaite is a multi-award-winning poet, playwright and dramaturg. Prizes include the Peggy Ramsay Award, Manchester Theatre Award, Theatre-Wales Award and the Ted Hughes Award for new works in *Poetry for Persians* (National Theatre Wales).

She is a two-time finalist in the International James Tait Black Prize for Innovation in Drama (2012, 2019). She was honoured in the 2017/18 International Eliot Hayes Award for Outstanding Achievement in Dramaturgy.

She was part of the creative exec' for the transmedia project *GALWAD* and the production dramaturg for Rambert's Peaky Blinders dance performance *The Redemption of Thomas Shelby*. Kaite's plays *Atypical Plays for Atypical Actors* and *The 'd' Monologues* are published by Oberon/Methuen/ Bloomsbury.

She is a leading figure in disability arts and culture internationally. Her first feature film, *The Almond and the Seahorse* with Mad as Birds films, will be released in 2023.

Hannah Marie Williams | Casting Director / Cyfarwyddwr Castio

Hannah is a Casting Director in Cardiff and London specialising in finding new and diverse talent, eclectic ensemble casts and exploring new ways to tell stories with the people who tell them.

Hannah's screen projects include work with BBC Film, BFI, Film4 and Sky which have gained critical acclaim, prestigious festival selections (TIFF, LFF, SXSW) and several BAFTA Cymru nominations. She was the Casting Director across live and theatre elements for *GALWAD* and cast the 10-part TV drama, *Carthago* which will be released onto a leading streamer in 2023.

Hannah has been casting for National Theatre Wales since 2022 and is the Casting Director for Frân Wen & Wales Millennium Centre for their forthcoming Welsh language musical, *Branwen*. She is also attached to several feature films including projects with production companies Spectrevision and Pulse Films.

Bianca Ali | Assistant Director / Cyfarwyddwr Cynorthwyol

Bianca is a spoken-word artist/singer, activist and domestic abuse advocate from Cardiff, whose poetry reflects on experiences she's lived. Bianca fights for social justice and believes in equal opportunities for everyone.

Bianca has appeared in local television shows as an extra, was Assistant Director on National Theatre Wales' *Circle of Fifths* by Gavin Porter, and is now Assistant Director for *Joseph K and the Cost of Living*. She has enjoyed being a part of the rehearsals and watching the show develop.

Cai Dyfan | Set and Costume Design / Cynllunydd Set a Gwisgoedd

For National Theatre Wales: *The Village Social, The Passion, On Bear Ridge.*

As designer, other theatre includes: *Violence and Son, Instructions For Correct Assembly* (Royal Court); *Paul Bunyan* (Welsh National Opera); *Croendena* (Frân Wen); *Trwy'r Ddinas Hon* (Sherman Theatre); *Sgint, Rhwng Dau Fyd, Chwalfa* (Theatr Genedlaethol Cymru); *After the End* (Dirty Protest); *Your Last Breath* (Curious Detective); *Wasted* (Paines Plough/Birmingham Rep).

As associate designer, other theatre includes: *The Lion, the Witch & the Wardrobe* (Kensington Gardens); *A Life of Galileo* (RSC); *A Number* (Nuffield, Southampton); *Mr Burns* (Almeida); *King Charles III* (Almeida/West End); *Medea* (National Theatre).

As art director and buyer, television and film includes: *Willow, His Dark Materials, Apostle, Dal Y Mellt, Hinterland/Y Gwyll, Y Swn, Wolf, Keeping Faith, A Discovery of Witches, Hidden/Craith, Born to Kill, Sherlock, Call the Midwife*.

Jane Lalljee | Lighting Designer / Cynllunydd Goleuo

Jane is a lighting designer based in Cardiff.

Upcoming projects include: *Song From Far Away* starring Will Young (HOME, Manchester), *The Card* (New Vic Theatre, Newcastle Under Lyme), *Rose* starring Maureen Lipman (New Ambassadors Theatre)

Recent projects include: *Aladdin* (Harrogate Theatre), *Constellations* (Stephen Joseph Theatre), *Right Where We Left Us* (Chapter Arts Theatre), *Rose* starring Maureen Lipman (Hope Mill, Manchester, Park Theatre, London), *One Man, Two Guvnors* (Bolton Octagon/Theatre by the Lake/ Liverpool Everyman and Playhouse), *Circle of Fifths* (National Theatre Wales), *I Wanna Be Yours* (Leeds Playhouse), *Grandmother's Closet* (Wales Millennium Centre), *The House With Chicken Legs* (Les Enfants Terribles/HOME), *Wind in the Willows* (Taunton Brewhouse), *Peter Pan* (Bolton Octagon), *Antigone* (Storyhouse), *Meet Me at Dawn* (HER Productions/Hope Mill), *Ghost Light* (Concept and lead artist at Ffwrnes Theatr), *The Storm* (M6 Theatre), *Dr Korczak's Example* (Leeds Playhouse), *Giraffes Can't Dance* (Leicester Curve), *Feathers* (National Dance Company of Wales), *Cotton Fingers* (National Theatre Wales), *Peeling* (Taking Flight), *Last Five Years* (Leeway Productions).

Alex Comana | Sound Designer / Cynllunydd Sain

Alex is a Welsh-Italian multidisciplinary artist and sound designer known for his unique approach to world-building. His work seamlessly integrates electronic and organic elements, resulting in immersive scores that are both otherworldly and familiar.

Comana regularly performs his compositions live on stage, treating the music as an integral and dynamic component of the performance. He has created work for Sky Arts, National Gallery of Singapore and Frân Wen, among others. In addition to his work as a composer for film and theatre, Comana also creates original electronic music under the moniker Miedo Total.

National Theatre Wales

National Theatre Wales is a free-range theatre company that exists to find and tell the most powerful stories of Wales and its people. A mirror and a microscope for all of us.

We're not tied to a building, which gives us the freedom to approach everything we do creatively, connecting people, places and ideas that spark stories into life.

We were founded in 2011 as Wales' English language theatre company, and our job is to create a nationwide community, welcoming people from all walks of life. TEAM; our approach to working with communities, is key to this. It opens up creative opportunities for people who may never have thought of theatre as something for them.

We're a registered charity (no 1127952) and we rely on the generosity of external donors to help us thrive. Our key funders are Arts Council of Wales and Welsh Government.

Everything starts with a conversation at NTW and we're always looking to hear from anyone who may like to get involved in supporting us, financially or otherwise.

nationaltheatrewales.org

Cwmni theatr crwydrol yw National Theatre Wales sy'n bodoli i ddarganfod ac adrodd straeon mwyaf grymus Cymru a'i phobl. Mae'n ddrych ac yn chwyddwydr i bawb ohonon ni.

Dydyn ni ddim wedi ein clymu i adeilad. Mae hynny'n rhoi'r rhyddid i ni wneud popeth yn greadigol, gan gysylltu pobl, llefydd a syniadau i ddod â straeon yn fyw.

Fe gawson ni ein sefydlu yn 2011 fel cwmni theatr Saesneg Cymru, a'n gwaith ni yw creu cymuned ledled y wlad o wneuthurwyr theatr a chynulleidfaoedd, gan groesawu pobl o bob cefndir. TEAM; dyma ein ffordd o weithio gyda chymunedau, ac mae'n allweddol yn hyn o beth. Mae'n creu cyfleoedd creadigol i bobl a allai fod wedi meddwl erioed nad yw'r theatr yn rhywbeth iddyn nhw.

Rydyn ni'n elusen gofrestredig (rhif 1127952) ac rydyn ni'n dibynnu ar haelioni rhoddwyr allanol er mwyn ffynnu. Cyngor Celfyddydau Cymru yw ein prif noddwr.

Mae popeth yn dechrau gyda sgwrs yma yn NTW, ac rydyn ni wastad yn awyddus i glywed gan bawb a hoffai gymryd rhan.

nationaltheatrewales.org

 @NTWTweets

 @NationalTheatreWales

 @NationalTheatreWales

 Cyngor Celfyddydau Cymru / Arts Council of Wales

 Noddir gan **Lywodraeth Cymru** / Sponsored by **Welsh Government**

Support us

Above all else we're about connecting people: because we know that connection brings the unexpected, opens minds, ideas, ways of thinking and outcomes. It's where creative sparks live. And by supporting us, you'll play an active part in these connections too.

Shared experiences are a powerful way to trigger positive change and we're brimming with ideas that you can help us bring to life.

As a charity, your support means that we'll be able to reach more and more people and help them to connect and tell their stories, all over Wales. We want to reach anyone who'd like to get involved – especially people who think theatre isn't for them – so we can show them that it is.

Your help is invaluable.

nationaltheatrewales.org/support-us

Cefnoga ni

Yn fwy na dim byd arall, cysylltu pobl yw ein gwaith ni. A hynny gan ein bod ni'n gwybod bod cysylltiadau'n arwain at bethau annisgwyl, at feddyliau agored, at syniadau, at ffyrdd o feddwl ac at ganlyniadau. Dyma sy'n creu gwreichion creadigol. A thrwy ein cefnogi ni, fe fyddi dithau'n cyfrannu'n weithgar at greu'r cysylltiadau hyn.

Mae profiadau cyffredin yn ffordd rymus o sbarduno newid cadarnhaol, ac mae gennyn ni syniadau rif y gwlith y galli di ein helpu i'w rhoi ar waith.

Fel elusen, mae dy gefnogaeth yn golygu y bydd modd inni gyrraedd mwy o a mwy o bobl, a'u helpu nhw i gysylltu ac adrodd eu straeon. Pobl o Gymru benbaladr fydd y rhain. Rydyn ni am gyrraedd pawb a fyddai'n hoffi cyfrannu – yn enwedig pobl sy'n credu nad yw'r theatr yn rhywbeth iddyn nhw – a hynny er mwyn dangos ei fod.

Mae dy help yn amhrisiadwy.

nationaltheatrewales.org/cy/cefnoga-ni

THEATR Y GRAND ABERTAWE

SWANSEA GRAND THEATRE

Swansea Grand Theatre

Swansea Grand Theatre has been a fixture of the Swansea skyline for over 120 years and has long been considered a stage for everyone.

From seasoned professional tours, passionate amateur groups, to up and coming youth drama, music, comedy and art, its diversity is a true reflection of our multi-cultural melting pot of a city.

Swansea Grand Theatre is owned and operated by Swansea Council.

Theatr y Grand Abertawe

Mae Theatr y Grand Abertawe wedi bod yn rhan o nenlinell Abertawe ers dros 120 o flynyddoedd ac fe'i hystyriwyd ers tro yn llwyfan i bawb.

O deithiau proffesiynol gan gwmnïau sydd wedi hen arfer â'u crefft a grwpiau amatur brwd i ddrama ieuenctid addawol, cerddoriaeth, comedi a chelf, mae ei amrywiaeth yn wir adlewyrchiad o'n dinas amlddiwylliannol.

Perchenogir a gweithredir Theatr y Grand Abertawe gan Gyngor Abertawe.

Cyngor **Abertawe**
Swansea Council

Joseph K and the Cost of Living

Emily is an emerging screenwriter and playwright. Before becoming a writer, she trained as an actor at RADA. In 2018 she won a place on Channel 4's 4Screenwriting Course. She was selected to be part of the BBC Wales Writersroom group 'Welsh Voices' in 2019. Her acclaimed play, *Pavilion*, premiered at Theatr Clwyd in 2019, directed by Tamara Harvey. In 2020 she was nominated to be one of the writers on the Nationwide Voices programme with the English Touring Theatre. She was also commissioned by Theatr Clwyd to write her play *Atlantis*, which won the George Devine Award in 2021. She has a TV comedy drama series in development with Little Door Productions and the BBC, and a film project in development with Riot Time Pictures.

EMILY WHITE

Joseph K and the Cost of Living

adapted from The Trial *by*
FRANZ KAFKA

faber

First published in 2023
by Faber and Faber Limited
74–77 Great Russell Street
London WC1B 3DA

Typeset by Brighton Gray
Printed and bound in the UK by CPI Group (Ltd), Croydon CR0 4YY

A CIP record for this book
is available from the British Library

978-0-571-38472-3

2 4 6 8 10 9 7 5 3 1

Acknowledgements

Special thanks should go to Lorne Campbell, Kaite O'Reilly, Kel Matsena, Anthony Matsena and Alex Comana for their help with the development of the play, along with all the performers involved during our development weeks and in the production rehearsals: Alia Ramna, Joshua Attwood, Mared Jarman, Rithvik Andugula, Gruffudd Glyn, Ioan Hefin, Sara Beer, Nevada Lemon, Rahim El Habatchi and Joni Ayton Kent; to our assistant director Bianca Ali, the producers Ruth Holdsworth and Glesni Price Jones; and to Bronwyn Wilson Rashad, our Wellbeing Coordinator in the rehearsal room.

Thanks also to Shahbaaz Shahnawaz at Trans Aid Cymru for their consultancy on the script. And of course, all the staff and crew involved at National Theatre Wales and the Swansea Grand during the performances.

This adaptation was written between October 2022 and March 2023, in collaboration with National Theatre Wales and Matsena Productions.

For Patti

my mum but also my friend,
who taught me to question everything,
especially authority

Joseph K and the Cost of Living was produced by National
Theatre Wales and first performed at Swansea Grand Theatre,
Swansea, on 17 March 2023. The cast was as follows:

K1, Leni Gruffudd Glyn
K2, Colleague 1 Joni Ayton-Kent
K3, Karla, Titorelli Lucy Ellinson
K4, Colleague 2 Kel Matsena
Ms Grubach, Block, Magistrate Sara Beer
Huld, Chaplain Ioan Hefin
Elsa, Cleaner Rahim El Habachi
Inspector, Tate, Glitterman Anthony Matsena

All other roles played by members of the company.

Director Lorne Campbell
Co-director Kel Matsena
Co-director Anthony Matsena
Dramaturg Kaite O'Reilly
Casting Director Hannah Marie Williams
Assistant Director Bianca Ali
Set and Costume Designer Cai Dyfan
Lighting Designer Jane Lalljee
Sound Designer Alex Comana

Characters

K1
the Joseph K we expect from Kafka's story. A cis white male from a privileged background. A junior analyst at a global investment bank. Solitary, isolated, inadequate but also arrogant and entitled

K2
a trans woman or non-binary person of any descent. For the purposes of this script, I use the pronouns 'she' and 'her' for K2 to be cast as a trans woman, but K2 pronouns and text can be altered to fit the casting

K3
a cis female of any descent

K4
a cis male from the global majority

Ms Grubach
Joseph K's landlady

Elsa
a burlesque dancer and a nurse

Karla
Joseph K's aunt

Leni
Huld's cis male assistant and carer

Huld
Joseph K's lawyer

Titorelli
a social media manager

Block
a female client of Huld

Prison Chaplain
chaplain at the cathedral

Cleaner
a cleaner at the courthouse

Magistrate
examining magistrate at the courthouse

Student
the Magistrate's apprentice

Guards, Inspector, Bank Manager, Colleagues, Whipper, Fruit Seller, Sex Worker, Preachers, Clerk, Water Seller, Petitioners, Volunteer, Glitterman, and other small roles

JOSEPH K AND THE COST OF LIVING

As neoliberalism wages war on social security and the public sector, impoverishes millions and destroys conditions of employment, its political consequences could be as disastrous as its economic consequences. In the 30 years following the Second World War, almost everyone in politics recognised that preventing the resurgence of fascism meant ensuring everyone's needs were met, through a strong social safety net and robust public services. But neoliberalism has stripped these defences away. In the gap between great expectations and low delivery humiliation and resentment grows. In these conditions, it is easy for demagogues to blame the frustration of people's hopes on scapegoats: women, asylum seekers, Muslims, Jews, black and brown people, disabled people, LGBTQ people, unions, the left, protestors. History shows that when political choice is lacking and people see no prospect of relief, they become highly susceptible to the transfer of blame. The transfer – attacking refugees and fomenting culture wars – is already well under way.

Excerpt from an article by George Monbiot,
first published 17 September 2022 in the *Guardian*

Notes

This play was conceived and developed as a piece of physical theatre and there are several movement sections in the script that represent a bureaucratic machine, fascistic in nature, that at certain points chooses a new Joseph K to persecute. The machine is in essence an interconnected system of state-led persecution that includes police, financial institutions, the media, religion and the law itself. Each transition comes from a different part of the machine: K1 police, K2 media, K3 church, K4 the law.

When they are not playing Joseph K or another character in a scene, the cast are still part of the machine, always watching, always listening in. Perhaps the actors playing K wear a costume marker that singles them out as the character and can be passed on to the next K, a red scarf, tie, or hat, etc., or perhaps they have a 'K' chalked on to their back during the movement transitions between Ks.

The Ks are four separate individuals going through a parallel experience. As such, there are similarities between their stories but the machine deals with them in slightly different ways.

Perhaps the character of the Cleaner shows up throughout the production, silently and meticulously cleaning, always unnoticed by the other characters.

All the choreography and music in the script are suggestions only and can be altered to fit the production.

A – at the end of a sentence denotes an interruption by another character.

A . . . at the end of a sentence denotes a trailing off.

A . . . instead of a sentence denotes the character is speechless for some reason.

A / denotes the overlapping of dialogue.

This play was still a work-in-progress when going to print so there may be differences between the script and the final production.

Act One

SCENE ONE

Music: 'Vessel' by Jon Hopkins.
All actors are somewhere on stage in a dilapidated
lodging house with many levels, stairways and doors, lit by
dim bare light bulbs. Industrial sound, a repetitive grind, the
oppressive crackle of a system listening in and watching your
every move: our machine. An automated voice does a
countdown, everyone stops what they're doing and looks up.

Voice Five, four, three, two, one. The market is open!

The actors stand and applaud. Gradually our city comes
to life. A movement section sets up the world we are in.
A world of order, of bureaucracy, the world of a lowly
junior analyst at a global investment bank with strict
rules and regulations, a high-pressure environment where
time is money and everyone vibrates with anticipation
every time their phone rings, a conveyor-belt system to
which everyone conforms.
Here we meet Joseph K1, a thin white cis man who fits
perfectly into this system. He is comfortable and content
to be a cog in the machine, working, eating, sleeping,
working, eating, sleeping. Until:
Morning.
In a small, cramped room with a bed, a table and two
chairs, Joseph K1 is asleep when . . .

Whole Cast (*to audience*) Someone must have been telling
lies about Joseph K.

K1 (*to audience*) For without having done anything wrong –

Two police burst through the door. A cockney Tweedle
Dum and Tweedle Dee.

Guards He was arrested one fine morning.

K1 Who are you?!

Guard 1 Who do you think?

Guard 2 starts to search his room, pocketing various items.

K1 I was about to have my breakfast. I usually have it at six.

Guard 1 opens the door a crack and calls to someone in the next room.

Guard 1 He was about to have his breakfast.

A short guffaw can be heard from behind the door. Guard 2 rips off K's bedcovers.

K1 Who's that?

Guard 2 No brekky for you today I'm afraid.

Outraged, K1 springs out of bed and pulls on his trousers.

K1 Does my landlady know about this? Ms Grubach?!

Upstairs Ms Grubach wakes and presses her ear to the floor. Some other tenants wake and group on the stairs whispering.

Guard 1 I think you better stay here.

K1 I will not stay here or let you address me until you introduce yourself.

Guard 2 (*offended*) He meant well.

Guard 1 I meant well.

K1 I'm getting Ms Grubach –

Guard 2 No. You can't go out, you're arrested.

K1 What for?!

Guard 1 We're not authorised to tell you that. Proceedings have been instituted against you, and you will be informed of everything in due course.

The Guards advance toward K1, Guard 2 towers over him, his fat stomach bumping against K1 in a friendly manner. Guard 1 starts examining his nightshirt, looking at the label and then in its pockets. The Guards strip the shirt from K1's back and then most of his underwear.

Guard 1 We just need to relieve you of this.

Guard 2 And this.

K1 Why?

Guard 2 No cause for alarm –

Guard 1 If your case turns out well, they'll be returned you toot sweet.

Guard 2 Much better to give them to us for safekeeping.

Guard 1 If you hand them to the depot they'll only be stolen and then you'll have to buy them back on the black market.

K1 What are you talking about? What authority do you have to –? Who sent you here? I live in a country with rules and regulations, there are laws in place, there are protections, how dare you barge in here and seize me in my own room.

Guard 1 Have you been listening to a word we've been saying?

Guard 2 He hasn't.

K1 This is a joke perhaps? (*He laughs.*) A joke played on me by my colleagues at the bank for my thirtieth birthday. A rude joke. Not a funny joke, but a joke nonetheless. Perhaps you're only porters from the hotel across the street and not police at all. (*To audience.*) They look like porters.

Guard 2 (*genuinely offended*) We are not porters.

Guard 1 It's no joke.

There is a tap at the door and Ms Grubach enters, with a tray of breakfast. She takes in the scene quickly.

K1 Come in.

Ms Grubach Oh. Sorry gentlemen, I did not know that you were here. (*She clearly did.*) It's time for Joseph's breakfast at six.

Guard 1 Yes, he said.

Ms Grubach (*babbling nervously*) He pays me extra you see, to make it for him. Coffee, toast and sometimes cereal. Coco Pops on special occasions. It's all above board I assure you, I include the payments on all my tax returns and have nothing to hide . . . um . . . I'll be off then Joseph.

K1 Stay Ms Grubach, these porters from over the road will be leaving shortly.

Guard 2 (*more offended*) We are not fucking porters!

Ms Grubach I'll just leave it here.

She puts a tray of breakfast down on the table and scuttles away back to her room to listen through the wall.

K1 Why didn't she stay?

Guard 1 She isn't allowed to, on account of your BEING ARRESTED. He's not getting the gist of this is he?

Guard 2 No he is not.

Guard 2 gets out a large knife, slices some bread, and sets about eating Joseph's breakfast.

K1 But how can I be under arrest?

Guard 1 Are you serious?

Guard 2 (*with a mouth full of breakfast*) We don't answer such questions.

K1 Show me your papers then. Where is the warrant for my arrest?

Guard 1 (*totally exasperated*) Oh good Lord! If you would only realise your position and stop being so annoying.

Guard 2 (*mouth still full*) He's worse than a child.

K1 Here. My passport. My identification.

Guard 1 What's that to us? We are humble subordinates and have nothing to do with your arrest, except to do as we're told and get paid for it.

Guard 2 (*quoting from the 'How to Be a Policeman for Dummies' handbook*) 'Our superiors don't go hunting for criminals but are instead drawn towards the guilty and then send us to deal with them. That is the Law.'

K1 I've never heard of that law.

Guard 1 All the worse for you.

K1 That law exists only in your own head.

Guard 1 He admits he doesn't know the law and yet claims he's innocent.

Guard 2 You'll never make a man like that see reason.

K1 I will not let myself be confused any longer by the babbling of wretched hirelings. Take me to your superior officer.

Guard 1 When he gives me orders and not before.

Guard 2 (*offended*) You have not treated us as you should.

Guard 1 We have the upper hand in this situation, not you.

Guard 2 All the same, we are prepared, for a small amount of money, to bring you a second breakfast from across the street . . .

> *Guard 2 holds out a hand for some money, K1 gives a disgusted snort.*

No? Suit yourself.

Guard 2 sets the butcher's knife down very carefully on the table in full view. The Guards leave. K1 is alone.

K1 (*to audience*) They've left me here. How odd. Why would they leave? I could run; run and hide. I could emigrate. I could – (*Notices the knife.*) I could slash my wrists. (*He shakes off this thought.*) Although why on earth I would do that, I don't know. (*He laughs.*) Why would I? Because two idiots with the intellectual poverty of a flea, are sat next door eating my breakfast? No, that would be such a senseless act that even if I wished to, I couldn't bring myself to do it.

K1 goes to a cupboard and pours himself a glass of whisky, downs it, fills the glass again, downs that and fills another.

K1 (*to audience*) To make up for my breakfast.

Guard 1 shouts from the corridor.

Guard 1 The Inspector is coming!

K1 At last.

K1 opens the door and is met by the Guards, who drive him back into the room.

Guard 2 What are you thinking of? You can't appear before him half naked.

K1 But you were the ones who –

Guard 1 Here.

They dress him quickly. The Inspector enters and sits at a table.
As the scene progresses the other tenants and Ms Grubach, press their ears to the door to listen.

Inspector Joseph K?

K1 Yes.

Inspector You appear very surprised at the events of this morning?

K1 I am surprised but by no means very.

Inspector *Not* very surprised?

The Inspector notes this down.

K1 I mean . . . May I sit down?

Inspector It's highly unusual.

K1 notices the Guards are looking around the room. They also step off the stage and start examining members of the audience.

K1 Please do not move or touch anything, those are my personal things.

The Inspector makes a note.

Inspector '*Personal* things.' '*Not* surprised.'

K1 I mean that I am surprised but when you get older, like I have today, you become hardened to surprises and don't take them so seriously. I don't suppose the whole thing could be a joke . . .? The whole building would have to be involved as well as you people so . . .

Inspector It's not a joke.

K1 But on the other hand, I can't recall the slightest offence that might be charged against me. None of you are in uniform, unless what you're wearing can be considered uniform, but really you look more like hotel porters. And more to the point who would accuse me? I demand some answers.

Inspector You are labouring under a great delusion. None of us have any standing in this affair of yours. You are under arrest, more than that we do not know.

K1 But –

25

Inspector Can I give you some advice? Think less about us and more about your own behaviour. Stop protesting your innocence, it makes a bad impression. And you talk too much, everything you just said, could have been said, using a lot less words.

K1 But this is sheer nonsense! I want a lawyer present. That's my right isn't it? To phone a lawyer?

Inspector I don't see what sense there would be in that.

K1 What sense?! What sense?! What, what, what kind of man are you?! No sense in calling a lawyer when I am under arrest?! You burst into my room, manhandle me, eat my breakfast, can't answer any of my questions, leave me to rack my brains for, for, for any possible reason and then tell me that it is *me* that makes no sense! It's enough to drive a man mad!

Inspector Alright phone if you want to. By all means; please. Phone.

The Inspector hands him a phone. The Guards and Inspector crowd around him to listen.

K1 No. I don't want to, now.

The door gives way and several tenants tumble into the room.

Oh wonderful! We have spectators! Go away! Get out!

They scuttle away. K1 closes the door. An awkward silence.

Come gentleman, we'll make a deal. I'll agree not to call a lawyer or to bother about the injustice of your behaviour and we'll put the whole thing behind us. Let's shake on it.

K1 holds out his hand. The Inspector ignores this and gets up.

Inspector How simple it all seems to you, but I'm afraid that can't be done.

K1 It can't?

Guard 2 Cheer up.

Guard 1 No need to give up hope, you're only under arrest.

Inspector I was told to inform you of this and now I've observed your reactions, that's enough for today, and I'll say goodbye.

K1 You're leaving?

Inspector Of course.

Guard 1 Time waits for no man.

Guard 2 We have other people to arrest not just you. (*Under his breath.*) Thinks he's the centre of the universe this one.

Inspector It's time for you to go to the bank now I suppose?

K1 To the bank? But how can I go to work if I am under arrest?

Inspector Ah you seem to have misunderstood me. You're under arrest but that doesn't mean you can't go about your business. You are released under investigation, and you can carry on with your life as if none of this ever happened.

K1 Then being arrested isn't so bad?

Inspector I never said it was.

K1 In which case why even tell me about it?

Inspector It is my duty.

K1 A stupid duty.

Inspector But it is mine. You're such a quibbler of words Mr K. No one is forcing you to go to work, I just assumed you would want to. In fact, I brought two of your colleagues with me to help facilitate –

The two figures emerge from the shadows. K1 is shocked.

K1 What?! Why?!

Colleague 1 gives an awkward wave.

Colleague 1 Helloooo.

Colleague 2 smiles like a shark and twitches.

K1 Good morning! I didn't recognise you. Well . . . we should go to the bank then. Come along. (*To audience.*) His smile is unintentional, but on the grounds of humanity, I won't mention it.
(*To his colleagues.*) If we hurry we'll make the next train.

Colleague 2 They're not running.

K1 A taxi then.

Colleague 2 (*takes out phone*) I'll Uber to the back of the building, there are protestors glued to the front.

K1 Again?

Colleague 1 I mean, I agree with them in principle, I just wish –

Colleague 2 They would shut the fuck up. I completely agree.

They all exit laughing at Colleague 2's hilarious joke. The Guards and the Inspector are alone.

Inspector Search the place.

Blackout.

SCENE TWO

A Banker creeps on to the stage with their finger on their lips and shushes the audience.

Banker He's coming! Everybody hide.

Some of the cast hand out banners and balloons to the audience. Someone switches off most of the lights, whispering can be heard and then . . .
LIGHT.

Whole Cast Surprise!! Happy Birthday!!

A camera flash goes off on K1 facing the whole cast with a cake, party blowers, streamers and balloons. Confetti drops on the audience. Cast lead audience in singing 'Happy Birthday'.

(*Singing badly.*)
Haaaappy birthday to you,
Happy birthday to you,
Happy birthday dear Joseeeeph . . .
Haaaappy . . . birthday to you.

During this Joseph starts laughing hysterically, the cast look uncomfortable.

K1 Very good. Very good.

Manager Are you alright?

K1 I knew it was a joke.

Manager What do you mean?

K1 My arrest this morning. Hilarious!

Manager What arrest?

K1 (*to audience*) He's so good. (*To Manager.*) Bravo.

Manager I have no idea what you're talking about.

K1 Oh um . . . it's nothing, never mind.

Colleague 1 pops a champagne bottle.

Colleague 1 Have a drink K.

K1 No thank you.

Colleague 2 We got you a present!

Music: 'Toxic' by Britney Spears.
A burlesque dancer named Elsa appears and dances through the audience to the stage as the cast of Bankers cheer and leer and record it on their phones.

Elsa Who's the birthday boy?!

Colleague 2 He is!

Elsa (*purrs*) Hello Joseph. Happy birthday.

Elsa grabs K1 and wraps herself provocatively around him.

K1 Er sorry, not today, thank you.

Whole Cast Awww.

Elsa Are you joking? I rushed here from my other job; I got a babysitter.

K1 I'm just not feeling . . . I have a lot of work to do.

Elsa I'm still being paid, right?

K1 Please. Carry on without me.

K1 exits.

Elsa I am still being paid?

Colleague 1 Of course.

Colleague 2 What's your other job sweetheart?

Elsa I'm a nurse.

Colleague 2 Check-ups all round!

Whole Cast Wahey!

The music swells as the Bankers cheer and surround her, waving twenty-pound notes at her. They freeze as a spotlight reveals K1 with his mobile phone to his ear, we hear it ringing and then:

K1 Hello? I wish to make a complaint.

An automated voice says:

Voice The police department is experiencing a high volume of calls right now. Please hold. This call is being recorded for training and monitoring purposes.

Blackout.

SCENE THREE

Ms Grubach is doing her accounts at the table. K1 knocks and enters. The room is identical to K1's.

Ms Grubach Come in Joseph.

K1 I wanted to apologise for this morning. For the men that were here.

Ms Grubach There were complaints.

K1 It won't happen again.

Ms Grubach (*sorrowful*) No. I'm afraid it can't.

K1 I'm sorry for the disturbance.

Ms Grubach Don't take this personally Joseph but if you weren't my favourite tenant I would be giving you your notice.

K1 I understand.

Ms Grubach Luckily you have always paid me on time and kept the place clean and tidy. Not like the others, secretly subletting their rooms and suchlike.

K1 No.

Ms Grubach Packed in like chickens in a factory farm some of them and think they can get away without paying me any extra.

K1 Do they?

Ms Grubach But not you. You've been no bother. No bother at all. And you've a respectable job, so I was surprised to say the least.

K1 So was I.

Ms Grubach As you have been so frank with me, I'll admit that I did accidentally hear just a tiny little bit. And your guards told me a few things.

K1 And?

Ms Grubach You are under arrest.

K1 Yes.

Ms Grubach Not as a thief or anything bad like that. But in an abstract way that I don't quite understand. Sorry if that sounds stupid.

K1 The whole thing is stupid. It is nothing but a figment, a mere trifle.

Ms Grubach What are you accused of?

K1 Ah well that's the thing you see, I don't know. Anyway it won't happen again. Let's agree not to give it any more thought. We should shake on it.

He holds out his hand.

(*To audience.*) Will she take my hand I wonder?

Suddenly all the lights go out, leaving only an emergency light. An automated voice comes over a speaker.

Voice Please put credit in the meter. Please put credit in the meter. (*etc.*)

The tenants start shouting.

Tenants Ms Grubach!

Ms Grubach Yes! Yes! Hold your horses! One second Joseph.

She goes to a microphone and speaks into it.

Would the tenant at 4B please put credit in the meter. It's your turn. Now please.

Tenant 1 But I put credit in yesterday.

Tenant 2 We all did.

Tenant 1 This is getting ridiculous.

Ms Grubach Put the credit in the meter or I'll put your rent up!

The lights come back on.

Not yours Joseph, don't worry.

K1 I'll say goodnight, Ms Grubach.

He holds out his hand again. She takes his hand with tears in her voice.

Ms Grubach Don't take it too much to heart Joseph. Lots of things happen in this world. Goodnight.

Blackout.

Telephones ring in the darkness.

K1 arrives at the bank to find protestors stood outside holding up blank banners. He picks his way past them, over and around them, a protestor grabs his legs.

K1 Can you let go of me please?

Protestor How much of your humanity are you willing to give up?

K1 What?

Protestor We can't go on like this.

K1 extricates himself and goes into the bank.

K1 I don't have time for this shit, I've got my own problems.

K1 sits at his desk to work but he hears strange sounds coming from behind a door. No one else in the office seems to notice.

(*To audience.*) Did you hear that? I think it's coming from . . .

K1 opens a door into a dimly lit room and finds the two Guards stripped to the waist, and a bare-chested man holding a whip and wearing a mask. The Guards cry out to him.
Whip!

K1 What the hell is going on?

Guard 2 Sir! We're being flogged because you complained about us!

K1 I didn't complain, I only said what happened.

Guard 2 If you knew how badly we were paid, you wouldn't be so hard on us!

Guard 1 We have families to feed!

Guard 2 And a man never gets rich from hard work, even if he toils day and night!

The Whipper draws back his whip.

K1 Wait! This isn't what I wanted!

Guard 1 Your fine nightshirt and underwear were too much of a temptation!

Guard 2 Yes it is forbidden. We know it was wrong, but it's tradition!

Guard 1 Body-linen is the warders' prerogative!

Guard 2 It is our inheritance!

Guard 1 We were good warders.

Guard 2 Now our careers are finished.

Whip!

K1 I never asked for them to be whipped! Is there no way for this to be stopped?

Whipper If I stop, then I'll get a whipping.

K1 Please!

Whipper You mustn't believe them. Careers?! See how fat he is? Do you know why? He stuffs himself with the breakfasts of all the people he arrests.

K1 Please you've punished them enough. I don't in the least blame them, it is the organisation that is to blame, the high officials.

Whipper Enough. I am here to whip people and whip them I shall.

Guard 2 If you can't get him to spare both of us, try to get me off at least. He's my superior, I was only following orders. I have children and a heart condition!

K1 I'll reward you! I'll pay you to stop! How much do you want?

The Guards get up unscathed and dust themselves down.

Whipper That won't be necessary Mr K. These events have been added to your file. Please return to your desk and await further instruction. Good day.

Guard 2 Laters.

Guard 1 Byeee.

The Whipper and the Guards leave. A spotlight appears over K1's desk, his phone rings immediately; terrified, K1 answers it.

K1 Hello?

The whole office stops and holds its breath to listen in.

Right now? I see. (*To audience.*) My first interrogation, I feel sick. (*To phone.*) Where? Yes I'll be there.

He replaces the receiver; the office comes back to life. Colleague 2 can smell blood in the water.

Colleague 2 Bad news?

K1 No, no, it's nothing.

Colleague 2 You sure? You look white as a sheet.

Manager enters.

Manager Ah K, I'm having a party tonight to celebrate my bonus. All juniors are invited to network. A good opportunity to really monetise those relationships.

K1 Thank you sir but I have a previous engagement.

Manager Ah pity.

K1 Next time.

Colleague 2 I'll be there, sir.

36

Manager Good. Glad to hear it.

Colleague 1 Where are you going? It must be important.

All the phones start ringing at once.

Manager Nearing end of day gentlemen.

K1 exits hurriedly.

Colleague 2 Power hour!

The banking floor erupts into chaos with Bankers making deals over the phone.

Bankers The FTSE 100 Share Index is at record peak.
There's still a hefty appetite for oil, gas and coal assets.
Fifty million at forty-seven and a half.
I'm telling you the only thing going down on you is the price!
The numbers don't lie.
Are you ready to buy some national assets at fire sale prices?
We've got Third World Debt for sale with sensational interest rates.

SCENE FIVE

A town square below a grey tenement building in a poor part of the city. A busker sets up a microphone and begins to murder a tune on an accordion. A homeless person begins to waltz to it alone. A Fruit Seller comes through the audience selling their wares.

Fruit Seller Lovely apples! One pound a bowl! Apples my love? No? How about a kumquat? Gorgeous they are. Only seven pound a bag. Yeah, I know. It's that Brexit. Terrible for business but at least now we dictate the shape of our own bananas. Am I right? No, no bananas at all I'm afraid. Supply problems.

A Sex Worker comes through the audience doing the same.

Sex Worker Handjobs, blowjobs, a tenner a tit!

A Street Preacher enters with a megaphone.

Preacher 1 The world is not getting any better! You can read it in any newspaper! Famine, war and disease! The world has cancer, and the blackness is spreading!

Sex Worker Handjobs! Blowjobs!

K1 enters looking lost.

Preacher 1 Children go to bed hungry. People are starving, people are freezing, people are burning, people are drowning! But I bring to you good news!

K1 Um hello –

Fruit Seller Kumquats!

Sex Worker A tenner for both tits! Buy one get one free!

A Preacher enters with a speaker and a microphone.

Preacher 1 You can escape the pains and hurts of this ravaged world. If you trust in Jesus.

K1 Actually I was looking –

The Preachers have a preach-off, getting more and more angry with one another until they're physically fighting, one bashing the other over the head with his microphone.

Preacher 2 Do not listen to this man! He's part of the Illuminati!

Preacher 1 Trust in Jesus!

Preacher 2 He works on behalf of the lizard people! They're sucking the blood of our young in Pizza Huts up and down the country!

Sex Worker Can I help you darling?

K1 I'm just looking –?

Preacher 2 Covid was a global experiment! Climate change is a hoax!

Sex Worker Do you mind?! You're putting off my customers.

Preacher 1 Jesus loves you!

Sex Worker Great, will he pay my rent?

Preacher 2 Lizards!

Preacher 1 Jesus!

Fruit Seller Kumquats!

Sex Worker Tits!

K1 Is this the courthouse?!

Everyone YES!

SCENE SIX

K1 knocks on the door, a very tired and harassed-looking Cleaner answers.

K1 Hello, I'm –

Cleaner Go straight through.

She mops the floor of a waiting room as K1 goes inside. The room is packed with people who stand with their backs bent over, their heads knocking against a low ceiling. All are holding numbered tickets. Waiting-room muzak is playing.

K1 It seems quite full in here already.

Cleaner Yeah.

K1 The ceiling's very low.

Cleaner We had to downsize.

K1 Who are all these people?

Cleaner The accused. Take a ticket.

K1 takes a numbered ticket from a dispenser.

K1 (*to the man next to him*) What are you here for?

Man I'm waiting for . . . .

The man looks at K1's mouth, and recoils, pointing at his lips. He sits looking at the floor.

Man Oh dear, oh, oh!

K1 Are you alright? Is he alright?

An automated voice comes over a loudspeaker:

Voice Ticket number fifty-six, please proceed to courtroom number five thank you.

K1 checks his ticket.

K1 Hang on a minute this can't be right?

Cleaner What number did you get?

K1 Thirty thousand, three hundred and twenty-four!

Cleaner It's the backlog. All the barristers are on strike.

K1 How long am I expected to wait?! I have a life to lead, a job to go to, I can't sit here day in and day out.

Cleaner You could come back a bit later I suppose.

K1 How much later?

Cleaner (*she works out the maths on her fingers*) About a year?

K1 Oh for fuck's . . . This is ridiculous!

K1 exits.
On the street a group of protestors has formed, holding banners that read 'Enough is Enough.'
Police sirens. A voice comes over megaphone:

Voice Protestors please disperse. Go home, this is your final warning. We have been instructed to use force. This is your final warning.

As the Protestors scatter, K1 enters bemused by what is going on.
Music: 'Rank & File' by Moses Sumney.
During the next movement section, the police enter in a huddle, holding riot shields and marching in formation. K1 tries to evade them but they surround him and close in on him until he vanishes completely. When they draw back, K1 has been replaced by K2, a trans woman, who is now wearing the red piece of costume that marks her out as K.

K2 Please don't hurt me, this is a mistake. I'm not a protestor.

Police Hands behind your head!

K2 puts her hands up and behind her head.

K2 I'm not a protestor, I'm on my way to work. My ID is in my handbag.

Blackout.

Act Two

SCENE SEVEN

The office is busy with workers when K2's Aunt Karla storms into the office, physically pushing people out of the way, and slams her hands down on her desk. K2 remains calm, grace under pressure: she has been expecting this.

Karla The family skeleton!

All the Bankers turn their heads simultaneously to look and then look back at their computers.

K2 (*coolly*) Auntie Karla, it's been so long.

Karla It is necessary, it is necessary for my peace of mind –

K2 If you wish to speak with me please keep your voice down.

Karla What is this I hear Joseph?!

All the Bankers stand simultaneously and look, then sit back down.

K2 (*to audience*) She knows not to call me that.

Karla You sit there staring out of the window! For God's sake, answer me. Is it true?

All the Bankers simultaneously shift their chairs closer to listen.

K2 That depends; what you mean? And my name isn't /
Joseph.

Karla Joseph whatever else can be said about you, you have always told the truth.

K2 Have a seat Uncle Fred.

Karla Very funny. Answer the question.

K2 From your tone I'm guessing that this is about my trial?

Karla I've been calling the bank repeatedly and they keep telling me you're busy.

K2 Perhaps I am. You're talking too loudly, Auntie. People can hear. There is a case but it's –

Karla And you sit there coolly with a criminal case hanging over you?!

The Bankers simultaneously jump and then lean in to listen.

K2 I have to remain calm in order to keep my position at the bank. I don't owe the family an explanation, I haven't heard from any of you in years.

Karla That's a fine thing to say! Don't you ever think of your relatives? You have put us through so much already and now you bring us more embarrassment. Your attitude doesn't please me at all, that isn't how an innocent man behaves if he still has his senses.

K2 Would you stop calling me that!

Karla Are you unwell? You look unstable. Perhaps it's time you went away to the countryside? Took some sick leave in a facility, away from prying eyes?

K2 Is that a threat? (*To audience.*) It is.

Karla I have allowed you your independence until now, I got you your little job and your little room, but your trial puts all that in jeopardy, and it is my duty to protect you.

K2 I never asked for your protection. I don't want it.

Karla That's not up to you.

K2 I have been doing very well without your interference. In fact, any problems I suffered in the past were a direct result of your treatment of me.

Karla Do you want to lose this case? Do you know what that would mean? You would be ruined. I would be ruined. The family name dragged through the mud.

K2 I don't see how the family name need be affected by a case against *me*.

Karla Oh pull yourself together! I can't afford for you to be so naive.

Karla ushers K2 out of the office and through various doors, the rest of the cast tiptoeing and creeping behind them. Every now and then K2 turns to make sure no one is following, and everyone freezes, hiding in plain sight. A bit like grandmother's footsteps.

K2 Where are you taking me?

Karla To the advocate Huld. A lawyer friend of mine. We were at Oxford together. Not a top lawyer but you are not in a position to be choosy. And since it is I that will foot the bill, I won't take no for an answer. Open the door! We're friends of Mr Huld!

Karla rings the bell. Nothing. Impatient, she rings again. A man's voice whispers in the darkness.

Leni Mr Huld is ill.

Karla (*almost shouting*) Ill you say?! Did you say he's ill?!

Leni opens the door.

Leni (*whispering*) Yes.

Karla (*barging in*) Next time be sharper opening the door.

Karla barges her way in and up the stairs, gripping K2 by the hand.

Leni Wait! Stop! Mr Huld is ill, you can't come in!

K2 Sorry.

Leni He's in bed!

Karla What's wrong with him?

Leni His heart.

Karla opens the door to a darkened room lit by candles. In the middle of the room is a bed with an enormous pile of blankets and pillows, and in it: the lawyer Huld, an old Etonian the size of a walrus, wheezing dramatically. Schubert's 'Ave Maria' is playing softly in the background.

Huld Leni? Who is it?

Karla It's your old friend Karla.

Huld (*wheezes loudly*) Karla . . . (*Big wheeze.*) Come in.

Karla Is this a bad time?

Huld A heart attack.

Karla I'm sure it will pass like all the others.

Huld This one is worse.

Karla I say, that is bad news.

Huld I'm losing strength daily.

Karla It's very gloomy in here.

Huld I had a heart attack.

Karla Yes you said. Are you being looked after alright? This boy of yours doesn't seem very bright. Took an age to answer the door.

Leni is studying at K2 very intently. K2 shifts uncomfortably.

Huld Leni looks after me. And assists me in all matters.

Leni goes to Huld and whispers in his ear, never taking his eyes off K2.

Karla (*impatient*) Will you piss off now please? I must consult my friend on some personal business.

Leni My master is ill; you cannot consult him about anything.

Karla Why you impertinent little –

Huld You can discuss anything in front of Leni, he is my eyes and ears.

Karla This is a private matter concerning family.

Huld So, you're not paying a sick visit but are here on business. You should have said. Go now Leni, be good.

Leni leaves submissively. Huld has stopped wheezing.

Karla You look better already.

Huld Your case is one that interests me very much.

K2 You know about it?

Huld I'm a lawyer, I move in circles where cases are discussed, the more striking ones stick in my mind.

K2 Who else moves in these circles of yours?

Huld Men of my own profession of course.

Karla Stop asking questions like a child. What's the matter with you?

K2 What about client confidentiality?

Huld But you're not a client. You have no lawyer.

Karla Which is why we're here! Will you pipe down?!

K2 I think I have a right to know who is talking about me. Do they know what I have been charged with? Because I –

Huld That information has not yet come to light. You have been released under investigation, but how long the investigation will continue and when your trial will take place it is impossible to predict, could be months, could be years. Your case may not be a priority to the police, but it will be to me, I have the power to make sure it's proceeding as it should.

Karla Wonderful! Say thank you.

K2 Thank you.

Huld Of course in the bedridden state I find myself, I don't have as many networking opportunities as I once did. I do however receive many visitors. There's one here right now as a matter of fact.

K2 Now?

There is movement in the corner of the room.

Who's there?!

A figure emerges from the shadows.

How long have you been there watching?

Huld This is the Chief Clerk of the Court.

Clerk I couldn't resist taking the opportunity to meet an old school friend. I was in the year below. We were at the commemoration ball together. Do you remember? Got completely sloshed.

Karla shrieks with recognition, they do an elaborate secret handshake and roar with laughter.

K2 Can we get back to –?

Clerk Fascinating case! Bound to be high profile.

Huld Yes. I've never had a trans client before.

Karla Oh it's all the rage these days.

K2 Can I –?

Clerk Very exciting for the firm.

Karla She'll be excellent for business.

K2 (*to audience*) And finally she gets it right. (*To Huld.*) So can I tell you –?

Karla Shh. We must listen to the experts.

47

K2 (*to audience*) Aaargh!

Huld Well what I can deduce, from the conversations I have had –

K2 Can I at least explain – ?

Huld It all began when the police burst in –

K2 Can – ?

Karla Is that so?!

Clerk You'll know the Chief Inspector actually, he was in my year.

Karla Really?!

Another roar of laughter from the three others. K2 gives up.

K2 (*to audience*) Oh for fuck's sake. I'll just go then shall I?

They ignore her. K2 goes out into the corridor and starts to explore the house.

SCENE EIGHT

K2 goes into another dimly lit room with a huge picture frame on the wall – and inside it an actor depicts a man in a judge's robe. He is sitting on a golden, high, throne-like seat and casting judgement. She gets out her phone and takes a photograph of it.

Leni Impressive isn't it?

K2 Oh you made me jump.

Leni It's alright. I'm not spying on you. Sit down, let's have a chat.

K2 sits.

I saw the way you were looking at me.

48

K2 What way? I wasn't –

Leni sits too close to K2 and stares at her intently.

Leni Call me Leni.

K2 I wasn't looking at you Leni.

Leni You didn't like me at first . . . perhaps even now.

K2 I don't even know you, I'm indifferent.

Leni (*laughs*) Oh!

K2 looks up at the picture on the wall.

K2 Perhaps he is my judge . . .

Leni I know him. He comes here all the time. That picture looks nothing like him, Photoshopped. He's a dumpy, squat little man in real life, but vain as hell, like all of them. I'm vain too, I suppose. It upsets me that you don't like me.

The picture moves.

K2 (*to audience*) Did you see that? (*To Leni.*) The picture, it moved.

Leni A trick of the light. I can tell you all kinds of information about him if you want me to. Others too.

K2 What's his rank?

Leni Only an Examining Magistrate.

He plays with the fingers on one of K2's hands. K2 notices but says nothing.

K2 But he's sitting on such a high seat.

The picture moves.

It moved again! Did you see it?

Leni Relax. You seem distressed. I can help you if you like? Would you like that?

Beat.

49

K2 Yes. Tell me about the Inspector in charge of my investigation.

Leni I'll tell you everything about him.

K2 Well?

Leni Next time. Once we've gotten to know one another better. Let's talk about something else. You're brooding over your case far too much.

Leni take's K2's hand. K2 notices but says nothing.

K2 Not really. I probably brood too little over it.

Leni I heard you were unyielding.

K2 Who told you that?

Leni I can't give names, so don't ask me.

K2 No names at all?

Leni shakes his head slowly. K2 kisses Leni's hand.

Leni Well perhaps some other time I will. A warning though. You must stop resisting and admit your fault. Until you confess there's no possibility of escaping their clutches.

K2 And if I don't?

Leni Then I can't help you, no one can.

K2 . . .

Leni Do you have a sweetheart?

K2 No.

Leni Oh, yes, you do. Don't lie.

K2 Well, yes I have.

K2 shows Leni a photo on her phone.

Leni I don't like him.

K2 Neither do I really.

Leni So he's not a sweetheart at all, only a lover. You wouldn't even miss him if you were to exchange him for me would you?

K2 I might.

Leni Why?

K2 He doesn't know about my case.

Leni That's not an advantage.

K2 It is to me.

Leni Any physical defects?

K2 Defects?

Leni Yes does he have any? I do. Look.

Leni shows K2 a scar on his lip.

My scars. A fist split my lip wide open. And my eyebrow here. Feel it. Not like you, you're perfect.

K2 makes a decision and kisses Leni.

Oh! You kissed me! You have exchanged him for me after all!

Karla's bursts into the room.

Karla There you are! Do you have any idea of the embarrassment you just caused me? You sneak away like a thief in the night to cavort with this lowlife when we have come here to plead for legal assistance.

K2 You were so busy talking over me, I didn't think you'd notice.

Karla Etiquette is everything. This is the dance we do, or have you forgotten? I only hope you haven't done your case irreparable damage.

K2 I'm sorry Auntie.

Karla There's a car waiting outside. Chop-chop.

Karla exits, K2 follows.

Leni Wait! What's your name?

K2 Call me K.

Leni Here's a key, come whenever you like. You belong to me now.

Leni kisses her and closes the door.
Blackout.

SCENE NINE

Outside the bank, but someone has sabotaged the sign to read 'Food Bank' and a table is being set up by a Volunteer with boxes of food to hand out to a line of people, Elsa among them.
A Water Seller enters.

Water Seller Get your raw sewage! Five pounds. Lovely bottle of water with sewage included at no extra cost!

Two Petitioners canvass the audience.

Petitioner 1 Excuse me sir, can I talk to you a moment?

Petitioner 2 You look friendly madam, it will only take a minute.

Water Seller Bottle of excrement madam?

Petitioner 1 I'm not asking for money.

Petitioner 2 I'm not asking for money, only signatures.

Water Seller How about you sir?

Petitioner 1 Sign here to protect our NHS.

Petitioner 2 Sign here for affordable housing.

Water Seller It comes with free chickenshit.

Petitioner 1 Sign here to support the workers' strike.

Water Seller Fully deregulated –

Petitioner 2 Sign here to ban zero-hour contracts.

Water Seller – fully privatised –

Petitioner 1 Sign here to stop sewage being emptied into our rivers.

Water Seller – and absolutely delicious.

Petitioner 2 Sign here to stop the deportations to Rwanda.

Petitioner 1 Sign here for rent caps.

Petitioner 2 For fair wages.

Petitioner 1 To tax energy firms.

Petitioner 2 To tax the rich.

Petitioner 1 To tax Rwanda.

Petitioner 2 For zero-hour housing!

Petitioner 1 To stop fair wages!

Petitioner 2 Ban the NHS!

Petitioner 1 Tax our rivers!

Petitioner 2 Introduce striking caps!

Petitioner 1 And affordable sewage rentals!

Petitioner 2 Oh and even if you don't have any . . .

Petitioner 1 Give us your money.

K2 enters on her way to work.

Excuse me miss can I stop you for a moment?

K2 I'm in hurry sorry, I'm late.

Petitioner 3 It'll only take a minute. I just need a signature that's all.

K2 No I'm really –

Petitioner 3 All we want is a wage we can live on.

K2 Fine. Here.

Petitioner 3 Thank you sister.

She takes the petition, signs it without looking at it and hurries into the bank. The Manager comes out of the bank and starts to argue with the Volunteer handing out food.

Manager What's going on? Who authorised this?

Volunteer No one did.

Elsa starts filming the altercation on her phone. Someone starts filming Elsa filming the Manager.

Manager You shouldn't be out here.

Volunteer Yeah I know. That's kind of the point.

Manager Move along please or I'll call the police.

Volunteer You'd call the police on a food bank?

People in the line start booing.

Manager You need to leave. Can you stop filming me please?

Volunteer How about a donation?

Elsa Yeah give us a tenner.

Manager I don't carry cash.

Volunteer Not even a tenner? At a bank?

Manager No.

Elsa How about that five-hundred-grand bonus then you fuckin' prick?

The Manager rushes into the bank to a chorus of jeers. Blackout.

K2 is stood in suspended motion as the rest of the office moves around her at speed as if they are on fast forward through their day and she is on pause.
The Manager walks past.

Manager You have clients waiting in reception.

K2 snaps out of it.

K2 Oh god I was busy, I forgot.

Colleague 2 They've been kept waiting for two hours.

Manager Two hours!

K2 The time got away from me.

Manager Our clients are important. They shouldn't be kept waiting at all.

K2 No sir.

Colleague 2 I can meet them instead sir. I think you'd be relieved wouldn't you K? If I took this off your shoulders? You seem so overworked.

K2 No I –

Manager Good idea. K seems preoccupied. Well done.

Colleague 2 No problem at all, sir.

Colleague 2 and Manager exit.

K2 (*to audience*) Shit.

K2 goes into her office. Titorelli enters.

Titorelli I have information for you that might help your case.

K2 Who are you?

Titorelli I am Titorelli! Social media manager extraordinaire! Your aunt, she pay me to learn you the rules of the game.

K2 Game?

Titorelli I have unofficial connection to the court. You will have seen some of my work.

He clicks his fingers and the company rush into a group and do a very cheesy TikTok dance video. Out of the middle of the dance struts an Andrew Tate-type figure.

Tate Welcome to the Players Academy, for men who wanna escape the matrix, make money, get women and defy gravity. I have the speed, I have the agility, I have the strength to be Batman. I am Batman but I'm also Morpheus and you can be too. For only fifty dollars a month I'll teach you how to have anything you want, anytime you want it. And if you don't believe me just look at all the cars and women I own. Are you ready to –

K2 I despise that man and his idiotic pyramid scheme.

Titorelli This is beside the point. He is the most googled man on the planet.

K2 Is that actually true?

Titorelli It wasn't when he said it, but it is now. This is how my campaigns work. Aaaand action!

K2 What? What are you doing?

Titorelli starts filming K2 on his phone.

Titorelli My first question to you is . . .! Are you innocent?!

K2 You're the first person to ask me that. Yes. I am completely innocent.

Titorelli And cut! Wonderful! Very good. I was convinced. But next time I ask, perhaps a little tear, a tremble in your voice like you are . . . *come si dice . . .? battagliera* the crying.

K2 But I really am innocent.

Titorelli Of course but who cares!

K2 I do. I want an acquittal.

Titorelli This is impossible. I have no influence of any kind over this. No one does . . . exceeept the royal family oooor if you are government minister.

K2 Then the court is a pointless institution.

Titorelli Oh you are so melodramatic! The point is we build you a brand. I write down an affidavit of your innocence. I do the round of the people I know. Judges, politicians, celebrities –

K2 Celebrities?

Titorelli Of course, I have 'influence' over many celebrities and your story in their hands, it would be so inspiring!

K2 But I don't want to be inspiring, I just want a fair trial.

Titorelli Fair?! Listen to me I am learning you. Perception of truth is far more powerful than the truth itself. For example! My name is not Titorelli, and I am not even Italian! I am. I'm not. I am.

K2 I don't understand.

Titorelli I am the inventor of truth!

K2 That sentence makes no sense. Something is either true or it's not.

Titorelli Oh you are so sweet but no. Leave it to me, I will invent you a reality that will make you famous. The campaign I can spin with you and your case, it will be front page news! You will be rich, magazines will queue up to interview you, every celebrity will want you at their party –

K2 But I value my privacy.

Titorelli Is too late, I post the video, everyone know your secret now already.

K2 looks distraught, Titorelli takes several photographs of her.

Bellissima! Hold it right there. Don't move.

K2 Stop, please. This is my life!

Titorelli You are not understanding me. Without this, your case, it is finish. So! I explain them your case, I myself guarantee your innocence. I get my celebrities to sign the affidavit. I take this sheet of signature to the Judge, notify the social media accounts that will be conducting your trial.

K2 No, I don't want my trial conducted by –

Titorelli This is the world we live in K! It is unavoidable. Everyone must have their say.

K2 And what happens then?

Titorelli I secure the Judge's signature also, and you walk out of the court a free woman.

K2 Really?

Titorelli Ostensibly. *Come si dice* . . . temporarily so.

K2 Wait, what?

Titorelli When you are famous the tide of public opinion is very changeable. One day someone will decide the charge is still valid and order an immediate arrest. Sometimes a long-time pass, sometimes you go straight home from court and find police waiting to arrest you again. Then, of course, we must create a second campaign.

K2 And a third, and a fourth and on and on into infinity!

Titorelli *Si.*

K2 But then I will never be free. I'll always be the accused and never prove my innocence. What about evidence? Irrefutable proof. Fact and fiction!

Titorelli What about them?

K2 But I want to live my life like anyone else, without restrictions. How can anyone be expected to live like this?! Knowing that any moment everything can be taken away?!

Titorelli What other options do you have?

SCENE ELEVEN

Music: 'I Decline' by Perfume Genius.
    The lodging house. Leni and K2 slow-dance, a stylised movement section, a moment of tenderness, a longing for intimacy and then:
    Leni is in bed. K2 is stood looking out the window.

K2 (*to audience*) Sometimes I get an overwhelming urge to jump. To fall five floors and be done with it. It would be so much easier. Not such a bad way to go. Flying. Don't you think?

Leni Come back to bed.

K2 The case is interfering with my work, I can't concentrate.

Leni Why not concentrate on me instead?

K2 Huld is useless. It's been a month and he hasn't cross-examined me once. Surely asking questions is the main thing? He hasn't even presented my first plea.

Leni The first plea is never read by the court anyway.

K2 Then why do I need his services at all?

Leni Because then it is necessary to file another.

K2 All without knowing what the actual charges against me *are*!

Leni Don't you like our visits?

K2 You're the only thing I do like about them.

Leni A convincing plea will come later, when we can guess what the charges are, from the questions they ask you during interrogations.

K2 Are you seeking to comfort me or to drive me to despair?

Leni Your defence is in good hands.

K2 He just sits there talking or writing in silence or gazing at the carpet . . .

Leni The carpet where we lay only the night before.

K2 Yes.

Leni Don't you enjoy it? The sneaking around. How I hold your hand and stroke your hair when he isn't looking. Don't you want that to continue?

K2 I . . . I'm considering drawing up a written defence and handing it in to the court myself . . . what do you think?

Leni What would you say?

K2 I would give a short account of my life. Try and explain in my own words every important event without sensationalism.

Leni It's dangerous.

K2 Eliminate any idea of possible guilt.

Leni To meet an unknown accusation, your whole life would have to be reviewed, down to the minutest detail, everything you have ever done would need to be examined from every angle. All the way back to childhood. You would be putting yourself under a microscope.

K2 I'm so tired.

Leni What about your position at the bank?

K2 I will never win my case by sitting silently in my office, letting others speak for me! I must be the one who speaks! I must be the one, and without shame! I will write my own plea.

The lights go out and only an emergency light illuminates the hallways. The lodging house springs to life with a cacophony of angry Tenants. An automated voice comes over a loudspeaker:

Voice Please put credit in the meter. Please put credit in the meter.

Tenants Not again that's the third fucking time today.
Ms Grubach?! Where is she?
She's out.
Has anyone got a coin for the meter?
Fuck the meter, I'm gonna rip it off the fuckin' wall!
Smash it to pieces!

The Tenants smash at the meter and try to rip it off the wall. K2 goes out into the hallway.

Voice Please put ten, twenty, fifty pounds of credit . . .
Please put three thousand pounds of credit in the meter.
Please. Please. It's not my fault. The prices can't be helped.
It's the war. It's Putin. It's Covid. It's benefit scroungers.
Homosexuals. Immigrants. The militant unions. The greedy strikers. The wokerati. The anti-growth coalition, those tofu-eating motherfuckers!

K2 What are you doing?

Voice It's them, it's them over there look!

Music: 'Grid' by Perfume Genius.
Movement section: the cast turn on K2 and chase her. They surround her and start to photograph her and film her using their phones. Everywhere she goes they follow, she tries to hide, to escape, but it is impossible. Finally, she pulls off the red piece of costume that denotes her as

K and throws it down, she is absorbed into the group
and moves with them in a shoal that moves in unison, all
alike, all exactly the same.

The machine singles out someone new, and throws
them into the space, but they push their way back into
the safety of the group. A game begins, a selection game,
or maybe more of a fight. Every member of the company
now knows they might be picked to be the next K and
they fight to stay a part of the machine instead.

In the end K3 is selected: a cis woman. The piece of
costume is put on her and she is picked up bodily by the
group and dumped at the door to Huld's office. She tries
to scramble back into the safety of the group, but they
spit her out again and dissipate.

SCENE TWELVE

K3 gets out her key and unlocks the door and goes in.

K3 Leni?! Are you in?! I need to speak to Huld!

*Block, a woman in a nightgown, enters holding a candle.
She has a shock of grey hair and hasn't slept in years.*

Oh! Who are you?

Block I'm a client, here on business. I work in sales.

K3 (*to audience*) Why is she in her nightgown?

Block Sorry, I'm half asleep.

K3 What's your name?

Block My name is Block. I work in sales.

K3 You just said that. (*To audience.*) What the hell . . .?
(*To Block.*) Where's Leni?

K3 pushes past Block. Leni enters.

Leni Oh I wasn't expecting you.

K3 Obviously. Who is this?

Leni Her name is Block. She / works in sales.

K3 Works in sales, I know. What is she doing here? (*To audience.*) Is she his lover?

Leni Come upstairs and I'll explain.

K3 You can tell me here.

Leni Surely you can't be jealous of Block? Block I'm under suspicion, defend my honour.

Block You have no reason to be jealous.

Leni I haven't seen you in so long. You've been neglecting me.

K3 I'm here to talk to Huld.

Leni He's very unwell today but I'll let him know you're here.

K3 Go on then.

Leni He might be asleep.

K3 Then wake him up.

Leni (*smiling*) You're so rude today. I like it.

   Leni exits.

Block So you're a client too?

K3 Yes.

Block I've been his client for a long, long time.

K3 How long?

Block It's difficult to keep track. Twenty years or so?

K3 Why so long?

Block (*intensely*) Don't tell him I told you that. I implore you!

K3 Why would I?

Block He's a vengeful man!

K3 Surely he wouldn't harm a loyal client like you?

Block Oh but I'm not loyal.

K3 What do you mean?

Block I shouldn't tell you.

K3 Tell me what?

Block Or . . . I'll tell you . . . but you must tell me a secret, in return.

K3 Okaaay . . . (*To audience.*) Bit paranoid.

Block I have . . . other lawyers . . . as well as him.

K3 Is that bad?

Block Yes! It is not allowed. It is forbidden. If he found out . . .

K3 How many do you have?

Block Five.

K3 Five?!

Block Six including him.

K3 Six!

Block And I'm trying for a seventh.

K3 Seven lawyers?

Block And I need all of them.

K3 Why?

Block I don't want to lose my case.

Block If it gives me even the faintest advantage I must take it. That's why I've spent every penny I own on lawyers. My offices used to fill the whole floor of a building, now I work from home. But it's not only the lack of money that shrunk my business, but the lack of energy. My case saps it all and I have none left to spare for other things.

K3 So you've been working on your own behalf as well?

Block I tried that in the beginning. But the results weren't worth the effort. I spent my whole life in the courthouse waiting room. But you know what that's like.

K3 How do you know that?

Block I was there when you were passing through.

K3 You were? What a coincidence.

Block Not really. You made quite an impression amongst those waiting . . . though of course it's all nonsense.

K3 What's nonsense?

Block Supposedly you can tell from a person's face, especially the line of their lips, how their case is going to turn out.

K3 And?

Block Judging from your lips you'll be found guilty, and in the very near future too.

K3 What?

Block You spoke to a man up there, didn't you?

K3 Yes.

Block He could hardly utter a word in answer because of the shock he got from looking at your lips. He said afterwards he saw the sign of your own condemnation.

K3 takes out a compact mirror and studies her mouth.

65

K3 I don't see anything wrong with my lips. Do you?

Block Perhaps it's your lipstick? Maybe you should take it off?

K3 removes her lipstick.

K3 How do they come up with these ideas?

Block I don't know. Perhaps while they're stuck in waiting rooms. The court won't allow them to discuss their cases you see, even if they have things in common. No combined action is permitted.

K3 No combined action at all?

Block No, it's *illegal* now, didn't you know? A new bill was passed in the dead of the night. That's why I have six advocates. You'd think with so many lawyers I could safely wash my hands of the case. But you would be wrong.

K3 So is it worth it? Has your case progressed?

Block Not that I can tell. If only I could employ one of the really big lawyers. The ones that always win. But ordinary people can never afford them.

K3 Who are they?

Leni enters.

Leni Look at the two of you putting your heads together.

K3 Leave us a moment longer.

Block She wanted to hear about my case.

Leni Well don't let me stop you. Carry on.

Block shrinks in her seat and says nothing.

He's waiting for you. Leave Block alone now, you can talk to her later. She's staying here. With me.

K3 Is she?

Leni She often sleeps here. Do you want to see her room?

K3 No I want to see my lawyer.

Block Sometimes he calls for me in the middle of the night.

Leni Sometimes Block has to wait three days for an interview, and if she isn't on this exact spot when he calls her, she's lost her chance, and I have to announce her all over again.

Block That's why I sleep here.

Leni Not everyone can get an interview with their lawyer at eleven o'clock at night, you know. God! You take everything for granted. Don't get me wrong I like doing things for you. I don't ask for any thanks. All I want in exchange is for you to be fond of me.

K3 He agrees to see me because I am his client, and he is being paid. If I needed others' help to get an interview with my own lawyer, I'd be bowing and scraping at every turn.

Leni How difficult she is today, isn't she?

They go to leave but Block grabs at K3's arm.

Block You've forgotten your promise to tell me a secret.

K3 My secret is, I'm dismissing the Advocate.

Block goes into a state of panic that gets more and more frantic.

Block Dismissing him? Dismissing him? She's dismissing the Advocate! She's dismissing the Advocate! (*etc.*)

Block runs a lap round the theatre shouting. K3 runs up the stairs to Huld's room with Leni pursuing her. She gets to the room and locks the door behind her.

In the murky mound of blankets Huld shifts like a mountain in an earthquake.

Huld I've been waiting . . . (*Wheezing.*) for you.

K3 It won't take long.

Huld Good. This is the last time I'll see you this late.

K3 Yes it is.

Huld Sit down. Why did you lock the door? Was Leni pestering you again?

K3 Pestering me?

Huld Yes. (*He chuckles.*) You didn't realise. None of them do. Which is good or else I'd have to apologise on his behalf. It is a peculiarity of his . . . one might say a fetish I suppose.

K3 What is?

Huld You look so bewildered my dear. Did you never even suspect? He finds accused women irresistibly attractive. Can't help himself. Makes love to them all.

K3 (*to audience*) . . .

K3 is speechless. The walls appear to be closing in as she fights a panic attack.

Huld He tells me about the affairs afterwards. A kind of bedtime story. Are you surprised? You look it.
It is odd that the fact of being accused should alter one's appearance so obviously, but it does. He has a trained eye. Even in a crowd he can pick them out. Of course, some are more attractive than others, but they are all attractive to him, even the most wretched ones.

K3 is struggling to breathe. The walls move in.

K3 I no longer require your services.

Huld Yes. Leni told me of your plans.

K3 (*to audience*) Oh god . . . .

Huld But I think it's a plan we should at least discuss.

K3 It's not a plan, it's a fact.

Huld We mustn't be in too much of a hurry.

K3 You keep saying 'we'; when it is my decision to make. Not yours, mine. *I* have made the decision! I have made it alone and I was in no hurry, believe me.

Huld At least allow me to comment.

K3 There's no need, I'm leaving.

Huld You are impatient.

K3 I am not impatient! I have waited and waited for something to happen, for you to do something, anything, but you have done nothing whatsoever.

Huld Many others have stood before me in the same frame of mind as you are now.

K3 I'm sure they have.

Huld I thought you would show better judgement. I have given you much more time and information than any other lawyer would give you and despite that you have no confidence in me.

K3 What will you do if I keep you on?

Huld I will continue with the measures I have already begun.

K3 Then we are wasting our time even talking.

Huld It is often safer to be in chains than to be free!

K3 What is that supposed to mean?

Huld Unlock the door.

K3 unlocks the door. Leni enters.

Fetch Block.

Leni Block!

Block runs up the stairs and stands outside the door unsure whether to go in. Huld does not look at Block but calls over his shoulder.

Huld Is that Block?

Block Yes, didn't you call for me?

Huld You always come at the wrong time.

Block looks at the floor.

Block Sorry.

Huld I saw the third Judge yesterday. We spoke about your case. Would you like to know what he said?

Block Oh please. Please.

Block gets down on her hands and knees.

K3 What are you doing?

The walls begin to close in again.

Huld Who is your Advocate?

Block You are.

Huld Besides me.

Block No one besides you.

K3 *(to Block)* What are you doing? Get up off the floor –

Block *(incandescent rage)* How dare you talk to me like that! Speaking in that tone isn't allowed in front of the Advocate! We are only here because of his charity. You think you're better than I am just because you're stood there watching me beg on all fours?! I might remind you that you are accused just the same as I!

The walls get closer. K3 struggles to breathe.

K3 We can leave together. Let's get out of here.

Block gets down on her knees again and crawls to Huld.

Block Please tell me what the Judge said.

Huld I don't know if I should . . .

Block Why?

K3 Block?

Huld What has she been doing today?

Leni She read the book you gave her. She did what she was told.

Huld But did she understand it?

Leni I doubt it. She read the same page over and over again.

K3 Block?

Block It was difficult to understand, there's so much legal jargon.

Huld Then you can see how hard a struggle it is for me to maintain your defence.

Block Yes I do. I do.

K3 Block come with me –

Block You shut your mouth when the Advocate is speaking!

The walls close in some more. K3 is physically holding them back.

Huld (*rapidly*) The Judge's remarks were not favourable. He was annoyed I even mentioned you. 'Don't mention Block,' he said. 'But she is my client,' I said. 'You are wasting your time,' he said. 'Block devotes herself to the

71

case,' I said. 'She lives in my house to keep up with the proceedings. Of course, she is tedious and deceitful but as a client she is beyond reproach.'

Block Thank you, thank you.

Huld Let me finish. He replied, 'Block is cunning but also ignorant. What do you think she would say if she found out her case had not yet even begun?'

Block stands up, shaking and whimpering.

Leni Quiet Block!

Block I must protest, I –

Leni If you're going to protest you must do it silently and without fuss.

Block shrinks back to the floor and is quiet. The walls are very close now.

Huld You must ignore the remark of the Judge, opinions differ, he thinks the case begins at one point and I another. Women are so emotional; they get into a panic over every word you say. Which is why I never tell them anything, and why you need me to protect you. Your final sentence is yet to come.

K3 Fuck this! I'm leaving. I'm writing my own plea, Block. You should too.

The walls move back.

Huld That would be a mistake.

Leni A woman with a history like yours, who will take you seriously?

K3 I'll report you.

Leni What for? The way I remember it, it was you that kissed me.

K3 Block and I we'll –

Leni No combined action is permitted. Block isn't going anywhere are you Block.

Block No.

Leni I know everything about you. Women like you need all the help they can get.

K3 How on earth could you imagine . . . could you believe, even for one second, that this performance would win me over? You're fired.

K3 exits, slamming the door in Leni's face as he tries to pursue her. She runs down the stairs and straight into the middle of a silent protest. People are stood silent, their fists raised, and their mouths taped shut.

K3 awkwardly tiptoes around them when a protestor reaches out and takes her hand. K3 is taken aback but the protestor looks straight in her eyes, imploring, looking for connection.

K3 . . .

For a moment it looks like K3 might stand with them and raise her fist, but she shakes her head, ashamed, frightened. She goes into the bank.

SCENE FOURTEEN

K3 sits at her desk writing her plea. Colleague 2 enters, slinks and prowls around her, spying, picking up bits of paper from the desk, reading them and putting them down.

Colleague 2 (*holding up a piece of paper*) Oh you made a mistake here look. She made a mistake!

K3 Do you mind? I'm in the middle of writing something.

Everyone turns to look. Colleague 2 gives his twitching smile. He reads over her shoulder.

Can you not . . . It's personal.

Colleague 2 Oh writing something personal on company time? I'd concentrate on these documents if I were you, they're riddled with mistakes. I'll show you how to do it properly. I'm showing her how to do it properly!

Everyone turns to look. Colleague 2 smiles again.

K3 It's fine. I can do it myself. (*To audience.*) Prick.

Colleague 2 Are you alright K? You look . . . unkempt. Where's your lipstick? You used to make more of an effort.

Colleague 1 enters.

Colleague 1 Your clients are here.

K3 reapplies her lipstick.

K3 Send them in.

Colleague 2 No I'm afraid there's no time. The manager has an errand for you.

K3 I can't run an errand. I have a meeting.

Colleague 2 I'll meet with them on your behalf.

K3 Can't I go later?

Colleague 2 No my dear K, this can't wait. We have an important client arriving soon and you're to show him around the city.

K3 But –

Colleague 2 If you play your cards right you might finally get that pay rise you've been after.

K3 A sightseeing tour? Why me?

Colleague 2 Because you're the only woman . . . who speaks Italian.

K3 But I don't speak Italian.

Colleague 2 How can you expect to be paid the same as us, if you're not willing to complete the simplest of tasks?

The Manager enters with Giuseppe, an Italian businessman.

Manager K there you are! This is Giuseppe one of our most influential clients.

K3 Hello . . . I mean . . .

Giuseppe immediately stands far too close to her.

Giuseppe *Buongiorno.*

Manager You two are going to get on like a house on fire K, I can see he likes you already.

K3 But I don't speak –

Manager Nonsense you're the perfect woman for the job.

Giuseppe We will start at the cathedral, no?

K3 No.

Giuseppe *Si!* We must confess.

Manager Meet him at the cathedral.

Giuseppe *Tra due ore. Si?*

Manager In two hours. Yes?

K3 Yes.

Giuseppe and the Manager exit.

If it's in two hours, I have time to meet –

Colleague 2 enters with K3's clients and ushers them into his office.

Colleague 2 Mine's white, two sugars.

Blackout.

Stained-glass windows throw light into the cathedral. The cast begin to sing the gospel song 'Sinner You Better Get Ready'.

Cast
  Sinner you better get ready
  Oh sinner you better get ready hallelujah
  Oh sinner you better get ready
  For time has come that the sinner must die.

They enter through the audience carrying flickering lanterns which they place on an altar inside the cathedral. One by one they kneel down and begin to pray till only one voice is left singing. K3 enters, wet with rain, and looks around for the Italian but he isn't there.
  The song ends. Only a muttered prayer can be heard.

K3 (*to audience*) He's late. These places give me the creeps.

K3 checks her mobile phone and sends a text. A rumble of thunder outside and the sound of rain. A Chaplain appears on top of the pulpit looking down on the stage.

(*To audience.*) If he's about to preach a sermon, I am fucking out of here.

K3 starts to leave.

Chaplain Come back here K!

K3 Me?

Chaplain You are K, are you not?

K3 Yes.

The Chaplain points to a spot directly below the pulpit. K3 stands on it.

Chaplain Then you are the one I seek. I am the prison chaplain. Why are you here?

K3 I'm here to show an Italian around a cathedral.

Chaplain No. You are here because I summoned you here. You are the accused.

K3 Oh.

K3's phone pings, she checks it.

Chaplain What's that in your hand?

K3 Um, I was just looking at a tourist guide on my phone . . .

Chaplain Put it on silent and put it down.

K3 Sorry.

Chaplain Your case is going badly.

K3 But my first plea hasn't even been presented yet.

Chaplain You are held to be guilty. Your guilt has been proven.

K3 But I'm not guilty. How can any man call me guilty? Every single one I've come across in relation to my case is corrupt and yet somehow I am the guilty one?!

Chaplain That is how a guilty woman talks.

K3 Are you prejudiced against me too?

Chaplain I am not prejudiced against you.

K3 You are prejudiced. You're all prejudiced. Even those on the outside who don't know the slightest thing about me, or my case, are prejudiced against me.

Chaplain Can't you see anything at all?! You have no understanding of the nature of the court you are serving!

K3 So come down here and tell me.

Chaplain I will not come down.

K3 Why? You don't have to preach me a sermon. Come down and sit beside me.

Chaplain In the preface to the Law it is written: Before the Law stands a doorkeeper on guard. A poor woman from the country comes to the door and begs admittance to the Law. The doorkeeper says he cannot admit her. She asks if she will be allowed to enter later. 'It is possible,' answers the doorkeeper, 'but not at the moment.'
So she sits and waits for days and years and during that time makes many attempts to enter but is always refused with the same words, 'It is possible, but not at the moment.'

K3 Why are you telling me this?

Chaplain The woman offers bribery of all kinds and she parts with everything she owns. In the early years she curses her fate, but as she waits and waits she slowly loses her mind, and even makes friends with the fleas on the doorkeeper's collar, trying in vain to bribe them too.
Finally her eyes grow dim, and as the world around her darkens, she believes she can see a radiant light streaming forth from the door of Law. As she is about to die she beckons the doorkeeper to her to ask a question.
'What do you want now?' asks the doorkeeper. 'You are insatiable.'
'Everyone strives to attain the Law,' says the woman. 'How can it be that in all this time, no one else has come here to seek admittance?'
The doorkeeper, seeing the woman is nearing the end of her life replies, 'No one else came, because this door was intended only for you. I am now going to shut it.'

K3 So the doorkeeper lied to the woman.

Chaplain It is not for you to pass judgement on the doorkeeper. He is a servant of the Law.

K3 But he didn't tell the truth. He had no intention of ever letting her in.

Chaplain It is not necessary for everything he said to be true, one must only accept it as necessary.

K3 This story turns lying into a universal priniciple!

Chaplain You have no faith.

K3 How can I have faith in a lie?! In a system that is rigged against me?!

Chaplain Where is your respect?!

K3 Where is yours?! I'll show my respect when it is earned and not before! This is enough to drive anyone out of their mind! This whole process is making me want to . . . sometimes I want to, sometimes I, sometimes I really think I could –

Chaplain Do it then.

> *The Chaplain exits. The robed figures surround K3.*
> *Music: 'Wish' by Anna Calvi.*
> *Movement section: the figures grab her and lift her up in what looks like a human sacrifice. They parade her around the space in what looks like a religious procession or ritual. They lower her body to the ground and she is swallowed back into the group. This then evolves into a dance of religious ecstasy with actors falling backwards and being caught as they convulse on the floor.*
> *The movement becomes more and more chaotic. Amongst the mayhem every person in the cast become protestors in a street riot, smashing and throwing things. Tear gas goes off. The cast scatter as K4, a person from the global majority, is pushed to the front of the group and abandoned. K4 is dressed in his best suit and ha, and is wearing the red costume marker. A voice over a loudspeaker shouts:*

Voice Get down on the ground your arms behind your back!

K4 This is a misunderstanding. I'm not a protestor, I'm on my way –

Voice Get down on the ground now!

K4 Please, I'm on my way to the courthouse, I'm going to be late.

Voice You do as you're fucking told!

K4 runs away terrified.
Blackout.

Act Three

K4 enters in a panic, he is holding his phone in his hand, using Google Maps.

Voice You have arrived at your destination.

K4 (*to audience*) There are so many doors. Am I supposed to knock on every one asking to be interrogated?

K4 knocks on a door. A man answers.

Man Fuck off out of it.

K4 (*to audience*) Charming.

He slams the door. K4 approaches another door and knocks. The letter box opens and the voice of a terrified elderly woman speaks out of it.

Woman Get away from the door.

K4 I just wanted to ask –

Woman Get away from my door or I'll call the police.

K4 I'm not going to hurt you. I'm going. I'm leaving.

K4 hurries to the next door.

(*To audience.*) Now I'm afraid to knock. But I'm so late what choice do I have?

He knocks and holds his breath. The Cleaner answers the door and . . .

Hello, I'm –

Cleaner Come in.

K4 Thank you . . .

Cleaner Go straight to interrogation room number three, they're waiting.

SCENE SEVENTEEN

The interrogation room turns out to be a large courtroom. The cast enter wearing masks and hand out more masks to audience members to put on; the cast then sit as spectators. Above them on a platform is the Magistrate. She is talking animatedly with the Student, a long thin man in a top hat, who is sprawled on a bench guffawing.

On another platform is a sound and lighting desk with a person controlling lights and sound.

An audience warm-up guy bounds on to stage wearing a glittery jacket.

Glitterman Ladies and gentlemen are you ready for the interrogation of the century?! I can't hear you?! Men in the room can I get a YO!

Men yo!

Ladies in the room can I get YAY!

Ladies yay!

Give yourselves a round of applause! Okay during the interrogation we're going to be holding up some placards and your job is just to do what the sign tells you. Got that? Have you got that?! Wonderful. Take it away Joseph!

K4 is shown into the courtroom by the Cleaner, who slowly and meticulously cleans the interrogation room throughout the scene, unnoticed, invisible. K4 is not entitled, but he is upright and proud. A man who knows without a doubt that he has been wronged.

The Magistrate looks at his watch.

Magistrate You should have been here an hour and five minutes ago.

The Student holds up a placard to the spectators/audience that reads: 'TUTTING'. The spectators tut loudly.

K4 I was held up by the protest, police have blocked off the street.

Magistrate That may be, but I am no longer obliged to hear you now.

The Student holds up a placard to the spectators/audience that reads: 'HEAR, HEAR'. The spectators: 'Hear, hear.'

Still, I shall make an exception in this instance. Step forward.

K4 Am I being interrogated in front of a crowd?

Magistrate Yes. Is that a problem?

K4 I thought I would be questioned in private.

Magistrate I don't know where you come from Mr K but that's not how we do things here, not anymore.

K4 Oh.

Student Where *does* he come from?

K4 Is that relevant?

Student It is if I say it is.

Magistrate I am obliged to inform you that everything you say and do will be captured on camera, so that people can make judgements from the comfort of their own homes. If you want, you can appeal for a private interrogation, but it prolongs things, and all the information about you will leak out anyway so there's little point.

K4 Leak out?

Magistrate We live in a digital age Mr K. Information spreads like wildfire, surely you've noticed?

K4 But what if the information is false?

Magistrate *Especially* if the information is false. But at least this way you are speaking directly to your spectators and not through . . . intermediaries. Do you wish to proceed?

K4 . . . Yes.

Magistrate Start filming please.

> *One of the spectators starts filming. Everyone starts playing to the camera.*
> *The Magistrate opens a large leatherbound book and thumbs through till she finds the page.*

Now then . . . I see that you are a . . . house painter?

K4 No. I work at a large bank.

Student (*snorts*) Doing what? Maintenance? (*Guffaws.*)

K4 I'm a junior analyst.

Student Oh, he's the diversity hire.

> *The Student holds up a placard to the spectators/audience that reads: 'LAUGHTER'. There is a heavy outburst of laughter in the hall along with canned laughter from the sound desk. The spectators are doubled up, laughing so hard they choke.*
> *The Cleaner starts to listen to the proceedings.*

Magistrate Silence! Order! Order!

K4 That question madam, about my being a house painter, doesn't that prove that there's been some mistake? My arrest, this interrogation, all of it, there has been an error made somewhere in the system.

> *The Student holds up a placard to the spectators/audience that reads: 'GASP'. The spectators gasp.*

Magistrate (*to camera*) That is impossible the system *does not make errors.*

K4 (*to camera*) If it's not an error then I have been *purposefully targeted.*

Magistrate (*laughs nervously to camera*) Mistakes are easily made! I can assure you that *we do not target individuals.*

K4 I am not a liar madam. I have committed no crime and have done nothing whatsoever to lead to my being here. On the contrary it is I that have been wronged and should be taking you and your officials to court.

> *The Student holds up a placard to the spectators/audience that reads: 'OOOH'. The spectators 'oooh'. The Magistrate thumbs through the book again.*

Since your book won't help you, why not ask me a question? This is an interrogation isn't it? Or perhaps now I'm not the house painter you expected, you don't know what to ask me?

> *The Student holds up a placard to the spectators/audience that reads: 'AAAH'. The spectators 'aaah'.*
> *The Cleaner surreptitiously steals a placard and writes on the back of it.*

What has happened to me is only a single incident, and as such, is of no great importance, but it is representative of a misguided policy which is being directed against many other people as well. It is for these people that I stand here, not for myself.

> *The Cleaner claps her hands high in the air.*

Cleaner Bravo! Bravo!

> *The Cleaner holds up her placard, it reads: 'APPLAUSE'. The spectators applaud. Canned applause comes from the sound desk. She puts back the placard and goes back*

*to cleaning. The Magistrate thumbs through the law
book awkwardly.*

K4 Put the law book down! For it is and has always been a
closed book to me. A man such as I could not even take it
in his hand. Could not even hope to touch it except with his
fingertips. For men like me it has always been just out of
reach. I see that now.

*The Student whispers something to the Magistrate, who
nods. The Student writes out a new placard.*

If you care at all about truth and justice then you will listen
to me! There can be no doubt that behind the actions of
this court, there is a great organisation at work. An
organisation which not only employs corrupt police and
inspectors, but also the media, government ministers, peers,
lords, perhaps even executioners.

*The spectator filming proceedings comes in for a close-up
on K4 and circles him throughout this speech.*

But what does this organisation want? What is its true aim?
I cannot tell you. All I know is the repercussions. Fear.
People are afraid of me even though I have never harmed
them. They feel hatred toward me even though we have
never met. And worse there is the fear that I must live with
day and night. That I will never be safe from their fear.

*The Student holds up a placard that reads: 'CUE
MUSIC'. Hollywood Oscars music swells under K4's
speech – his speech is being cut short. K4 tries to
continue but must now shout to compete with
the music.*

The repercussions are that innocent men and women,
instead of being fairly examined, are humiliated in front of
their friends and peers, and bundled into the backs of police
vans. Some never to return. I am here for those people, for
the disappeared, I am here to expose the –

Magistrate Enough! You may not yet have become aware of the fact, but it is an honour and a privilege to be able to stand in this courtroom. In fact, you have been afforded many privileges, which of course you have taken for granted.

K4 Am I supposed to be grateful that I was arrested for no reason? Grateful that I am stopped and searched on almost a weekly basis?

Magistrate Yes! This great country has given you so much but all you do is criticise, blame and denigrate! This is not the way to conduct yourself in an interrogation!

K4 An interrogation?! The only questions you've asked me are where my people are from and whether I'm a fucking house painter!

Magistrate WE DO NOT NEED TO ASK YOU ANYTHING! There is nothing you can tell us we don't already know! We know where you live, where you work, where you keep your money, we know your hopes, dreams, fears, friends, family, how many lovers you've had, their names and addresses, what you buy, what you read, what you listen to, how you vote, the petitions you've signed, the protests you've been to, we know more about you than you know about yourself. Data is knowledge and knowledge is power, and you give it to us so willingly. No piece of information is private from us because you carry your own surveillance around with you in your pocket. You hold it in your hand, it wakes you up in the morning and it's the last thing you look at before you go to bed at night.

And now it is my duty to inform you that you have just thrown away with your own behaviour, any chance you may have had. Good day Mr K.

The Magistrate exits, followed by all the spectators in the courtroom muttering 'Hear, hear' etc.

K4 Wait! Where are you going? What happens now?

Student Go home and await further instructions.

The Student exits.

K4 But how long is this going to go on for?! How long must I wait?!

The Cleaner finishes polishing something, switches off the lights and exits. K4 starts to have a panic attack. He is struggling to breathe.

How do I get out of here?! I don't know the way out! Come back!

Music: '20 Ghosts III' by Nine Inch Nails.

Movement section: K4 lurches up and down stairways around corridors opening and closing doors. Each room contains masked cast members that pursue him, everyone watching and leering, as they snake out of the rooms, grabbing at him as he escapes them, terrified. He runs out into the middle of the space and runs on the spot, but the other actors grab at his arms and legs and slow down his movement till it looks like he is running through treacle.

K4 escapes them and runs at speed but gradually his body begins to break and collapse till he hits the ground. He gets back up, it happens again, he gets back up and it happens again.

The other three Ks enter and run around the set looking for a way out; whilst searching, they stumble across one another.

Do you know the way out?

K2 No. I'm lost.

K3 Try this way.

K1 It's not down there I already tried it.

K3 How long have I been in here?!

K2 Hello?!

K4 Help?!

They wander into the centre of the stage. Four individual spotlights slam on, over each of them, with a massive clanking sound. They stop running, exhausted.
Some figures dressed in black wearing top hats enter.

K1 So, the day has finally come.

K3 Have you been appointed to take us?

The figures bow.

K2 Am I to be spirited away under cover of darkness? Unseen. As if I never existed.

K4 Where are you taking us?

K1 I only ask that you do not –

K3 Do not handcuff me –

K2 Until we are out of the building –

K4 Please leave me my dignity.

The figures lead all the Ks up to a platform.

All Where are we going?

K1 (*to audience*) I notice how clean their faces are . . .

K2 (*to audience*) They have scrubbed so hard I can see red marks.

K4 (*to audience*) But looks can be deceiving.

K3 (*to audience*) I wonder how long they had to wash their hands.

K1 I'll go no further!

K2 Even if I have to expend all my strength. I'll go no further.

K4 (*to audience*) I'm reminded of a fly stuck to fly-paper, ripping its own legs and wings off to get free.

K2 I always wanted –

K3 To snatch at the world –

K4 With twenty hands.

K1 Was that wrong?

K4 Was that a crime?

K3 Must I be punished for this?

K4 Someone must bear witness. A brother? A neighbour?

K1 Is that you Ms Grubach?

K2 Leni are you watching?

K3 Is anyone there? Or am I talking to myself?

K1 I think I see a human figure, faint in the distance . . .

K2 Who is it?

K4 A friend? Someone who sympathises?

K3 Someone who wants to help?

K2 Is it one person only, or are there many?

K4 Someone has been telling lies about us.

K1 Someone has been telling lies.

The figures push the Ks onto their knees.

K4 Wait. I'm not ready.

K2 Where is the judge that I have never seen?

K3 Where is the high court I have never entered?

K1 Someone has been telling lies.

The figures hand each K a large knife identical to the one in Scene One and exit, leaving them alone.

K4 What is expected of us?

K1 Are we meant to use these?

K2 On ourselves or on each other?

K3 Is that what they mean by necessary? Is that what they demand from us? Total submission? Like a dog?

K2 (*throwing down the knife*) No.

K4 (*throwing down the knife*) No.

K3 (*throwing down the knife*) No.

K1 (*throwing down the knife*) No.

K3 No, I will not. (*Raises fist.*)

K2 I will not submit. (*Raises fist.*)

K4 I will not submit. (*Raises fist.*)

K1 I will not. (*Raises fist.*)

An image of solidarity and resistance.

All Someone has been telling lies –

Blackout.
    The sound of the plug being pulled and a broadcast signal interruption.
    The End.